DARE TO DANCE

A Midlife Memoir

BETTINA DEDA

Dare to Dance
A Midlife Memoir

by Bettina Deda

Published 2022 by
VPI Publishing Solutions -
Markus Betzmeier-Wadams, Munich, Germany

Cover, Cover Image, Design and Typeset by
VPI Publishing Solutions

Printed and bound in Germany

1st Edition

ISBN 978-3-9818122-4-4

<u>To Mum.</u>
For you at last.

"Choosing to live and love with our whole hearts is an act of defiance. You're going to confuse, piss off, and terrify lots of people–including yourself. One minute you pray the transformation stops, and the next minute you'll pray that it never ends. You'll also wonder how you can feel so brave and so afraid at the same time."

Brené Brown, The Gifts of Imperfections.

CONTENTS

"Women have huge expectations placed upon them in life to conform to what others think they should be - as daughters, mothers, lovers. I applaud Bettina Deda for writing a powerful and honest book that speaks about making decisions based on our own truth, and the transformational joy in all its many and magnificent forms that comes from that."

Lliane Clarke, Artistic Director, Voices of Women

PREFACE

I had no idea that a massage could change my life, but that was exactly what happened on the 31st December 2016. It was a 90-minute dance that opened a mysterious door to a new world – unknown and frightening but full of potential. After I had returned from what was supposed to be a week of relaxation at my favourite wellness retreat in the hinterland of Byron Bay, I found myself in a vortex of insecurities which tormented my life on a daily basis. My mind replayed the same 90-minutes over and over again. A 90-minute dance that had turned my life upside down, became the catalyst for change and the reason why I wrote this book.

With every day that passed, I realised that many chapters in my life had come to an end. At the same time, a new path was emerging; I didn't know where it would lead me. Rather than hurtling through my days, I started feeling my way through each day, each hour, each moment. I reflected on my life and wondered how it would have unfolded if the year 1998 had not robbed me so cruelly of the two most important women in my life. Would I still live in Germany, the country where I was born and grew up in?

In 2008, however, I had the courage to listen to an inner voice that I had shut down for many years. I moved with my husband and sons to Australia to start a new chapter of my life. The land Down Under treated me well. Australia provided the fertile ground for my spiritual journey and personal growth. But, most importantly, it gave me the gift of reconnecting with my feminine wisdom, to listen to my heart rather than my head and to finally speak my truth. It helped me rediscover my creative soul and what would become my greatest passion: ballroom dancing, which I started aged 52.

One thing I discovered about myself is that for most of my adult life, I lived in my head, not in my heart. I forgot how to connect to my soul, how to tap into my feminine energy and intuition. I lived mainly in 'doing' mode instead of being in the present moment. This energy of tapping into my soul, my passion, desires, and fears remained elusive to me for many years.

"Stop thinking. Relax and dance from your heart," I heard my instructor say many times. On the dance floor, too much thinking prevents us from 'feeling' the music and expressing our creativity. I am still struggling with this concept, especially when I learn new steps or new layers of technique. It is a fine balance of surrendering to the music on one hand, concentrating on the steps of each dance and to execute them beautifully on the other.

One evening in November 2019 I discovered something else that I learned from dancing. I was sitting in the B-Line bus on my way home from a social night at the dance school. As often after dancing, the gratitude I felt in my heart made me emotional and teary.

On that night, I noticed that dancing is a great metaphor for every-day life and what I was looking for in a romantic relationship: respect, trust, and communication. Despite the fact that one person leads and the other follows, 'dancing is a partnership, not a dictatorship,' as the teachers used to point out. The dance frame connects the partners, each respects the space of the other, and the leader communicates with the follower through the frame. The goal is to move as one entity across the floor, graceful, energetic, and without changing the frame, while making it look effortless. I realised how often in my marriage I had not set the frame of how I wanted to be treated, in other words, boundaries, and thus paved the way for misunderstandings, resentment, and conflict.

Above all, dancing is a beautiful art form. If you are one of those people who always wanted to dance (or follow any other passion) and haven't done it yet, I invite you to take the plunge, to open that door to the unknown and to explore what you can create and become when you step out of your comfort zone.

To dance means to create beauty for myself and others. Whether on the dance floor or in my business, I am on a mission to inspire women to celebrate midlife, to listen to their hearts and find their passions. If you are one of those people who always wanted to dance (or take up any other new hobby) and keep waiting for that perfect day, I invite you to take the plunge.

I invite you to dare to dance, to come along with me on my journey of exploration and transformation in midlife.

A CONVERSATION WITHOUT WORDS

"Whatever happens to you has been waiting to happen since the beginning of time. The twining strands of fate wove both of them together: your own existence and the things that happen to you."

Marcus Aurelius, Meditations

*****

'Thanks for the dance,' Jay smiled at me.

I knew I would need to get up, put on my robe and slippers and leave the room where I had just experienced the most wonderful massage. Two days ago I didn't even know what Kahuna meant; now I could still feel his fingers, wrists and forearms all over my body. Over 90 minutes, Jay had touched my heart and soul in a way that no-one else had ever done before. And I just didn't want to believe that it was all over. Let alone think of the next morning when I would leave the retreat to return with my husband to our life in Sydney.

It was the 31st December 2016, the last day of a year which had been challenging in many respects, with me entering the unravelling phase of midlife.

Two days before, Jay had come into my life out of the blue. Together with my husband, we had booked a relaxation massage for couples and shared the same treatment room. Jay introduced himself as my therapist and I was smitten by his charms and his smiling eyes, when he kneeled down in front of me and asked with his soft voice if I was Bettina. The following massage was different from any other I had previously experienced.

Once the treatment was finished, I could still feel his hands on my skin. I couldn't stop thinking about him. Who was he? What had he done to make this massage so different from any other?

I finally decided to ask the spa manager.

'You know yesterday, I had this relaxation massage. It was so different from any other I had before. I can't remember the name of the guy.'

She quickly checked her computer. 'It was Jay, he specialises in Kahuna.'

'Kahuna?' I had no idea what that meant but knew that I wanted to book one.

'I'd like to book one before I leave. By the way, when did you book me in for the hot stone massage I had requested as additional treatment?'

She looked at her screen again.

'I am so sorry, I can't find you on tomorrow's schedule. We better book you in right now.'

'Hang on,' I seized the opportunity, 'Will Jay be in tomorrow?

'Yes, he is in tomorrow.'

'And would it be possible to book a Kahuna massage instead of the Hot Stone?'

'Let's have a look. He is pretty much booked out.' Her eyes scanned the computer screen.

I could feel my heart pounding in my chest and prayed that there would be a spot left for me.

'2 o'clock?'

'Sure, no problem,' I replied without hesitation.

I left the spa in anticipation of the next day. A short internet search revealed more details about the Kahuna massage style. I learned that it originates from Hawaii – the word meaning 'wise man' or 'shaman' – and is an ancient massage, traditionally performed to honour the body as a temple. It is used as a healing modality in rite of passage ceremonies. With a mix of rhythm, dance, music, and massage, Kahuna aims to relax, rebalance and invigorate the mind, body and spirit.

The next day, when the time had finally come, I changed into my robe and wandered through the tropical gardens to the spa complex. The manager asked me to sit down in the waiting area. Two English ladies joined me and we started a conversation about the weather, the heat and what sort of treatment we were waiting for.

Suddenly, the door of the staff room opened and Jay appeared. As always, he was wearing the spa uniform, a pair of wide-legged, flowing brown pants and a brown short-sleeve t-shirt with his long beaded necklace. He never seemed to wear shoes when working. I had noticed two days ago that he was the only therapist walking around bare feet. His toe nails were embellished with a light blue nail polish.

He stopped in front of the three of us.

'Hello ladies, are you waiting for your next appointment?'

'Yes,' we replied in unison.

'Well, I am confiscating this woman,' he grinned from one ear to the other looking at me.

My heart seemed to jump out of my chest. I quickly got up and followed him in one of the treatment rooms.

Once the door closed, Jay offered me a seat and smiled: 'Welcome back!'

I had to gather all my courage to tell him what I had prepared.

'I was so impressed by your massage on Thursday. It was different to anything else I have experienced before. Half the time I spent figuring out what you were doing. I felt such a deep connection to you although I don't know you at all. I believe you have a very special gift to connect with your clients. And when I learned that you specialise in Kahuna, I asked at reception if they could book me in today. I got a spot, so I think it was meant to be,' the words tumbled out of my mouth.

'That's interesting. Saturday is the only other day I work here. And thank you for the compliment,' he said still smiling.

'I read a bit about Kahuna massages, and I love music, dance and rhythm.'

'Well, you can massage many muscles in the body. The main difference to other massages is that Kahuna comes from the heart,' and his right hand touched his heart. 'If your mind is as busy as mine, the best thing is to relax. My hands will be all over your body while I am moving around the table. You will hear me breathing. This is my altar,' he smiled and touched the massage bed. 'I will listen and talk to your Goddess; and she will tell me what to do.'

I tried to digest what he had just said, it sounded mysterious, almost other-worldly, and he kept going.

'I will start with your back, your legs and arms and then ask you to turn around to massage your head, face and the front of your body, your chest, belly, arms and legs,' he explained the Hawaiian massage style further. 'If you feel uncomfortable with anything I do, please let me know at any time.'

I noticed that there was no towel on the massage bed. 'Do I lie on the bed without a towel?

'Yep, I will put oil on the bed, as I will also go under your body,' and he demonstrated one of the Kahuna under-body moves.

'Kahuna massages are usually done naked but let me know if you are not happy with this.'

'That's fine, no problem,' I heard myself say before I could even think about my words.

'Perfect, I'll leave you to get ready and be back shortly.'

I took off my robe and underpants, climbed on the massage table, face down, and covered my back with the sarong that he had prepared for me. Not long after, Jay returned.

He changed the music to a more rhythmic beat. I felt the sarong being lifted from my back and he placed a towel over my bottom and tucked it between my legs. He lifted my legs slightly and moved them apart so that my knees touched the edges of the massage bed.

Following his instructions, I concentrated on my breathing to relax. Then, I could feel the warm oil on my skin, his hands, forearms and elbows moving over my lower back making their way to my upper back, my arms and legs. After a while, I gave up thinking about where he was and what he was doing and surrendered to the rhythm of the music and his dance. I felt uplifted and grounded at the same time. At some point, he asked me to turn around, and the massage continued on my head and face.

'Bettina, are you happy for me to massage your chest?' He was touching my shoulders with both hands, and I could hear his voice very close to my ear. Without opening my eyes and mouth, all I could articulate was 'Mmh' and I succumbed again to this spiritual dance he had seduced me into.

I heard him get up from his stool and felt how the sarong was slowly lifted from my upper body. His hands touched my chest to slide down between my breasts to my belly and up again. The same dance he had performed on my back was now unfolding on the front of my body. I had completely lost any sense of time and enjoyed every second in this other-worldly wonderland of passion and compassion. In rhythmic movements, he followed the form of my body triggering feelings of total surrender, vulnerability and happiness in me.

I again felt this deep level of trust and connection to this man I hardly knew. And I could sense that he intuitively answered my unspoken words with his hands, connecting from his heart to mine, dancing with my Goddess, talking to her without words. An experience beyond anything else I had ever encountered. By no means, did I want this dance to end.

But then, his movements stopped. He covered me with the sarong and held me still with one hand under my head and one hand under my sacrum. I had no idea how long this lasted, all I knew was that our dance had come to an end with soft music playing in the background. I lay still, floating in a sea of kindness, compassion, and love; in this moment, I knew that I would never forget this man, who now seemed to know me better than anyone else.

Eventually, he lightly pressed his palms on my head, chest, belly, knees and feet and finished with touching my navel area.

He removed the towel from my eyes and sprayed a refreshing toner on my face.

'It is time to wake up and come back to the room,' his soft voice reminded me of the end of my treatment.

I slowly opened my eyes, reluctantly, something in me resisting, not wanting to come back to reality, not wanting to leave this wonderful place I had just discovered. I tried to make sense of what had just happened. A futile attempt.

'How do you feel?' Jay broke the silence, his green eyes sparkling.

'Good,' was all my lips could form. The mist of the rose-scented spray was still lingering on my face. My body still seemed to float lightly above the bed. Streams of energy inside me made me feel warm and loved.

Jay's spa uniform looked as neat and tidy as usual, the beaded necklace swaying lightly on his chest.

'Thanks for the dance. Take your time, I will meet you outside.'

A few minutes later, he served me a small timber tray with tea and bite-sized pieces of papaya, orange, melon and grapes.

'How do you feel?' He asked kneeling beside my chair.

'Peaceful' was the one word that popped into my confused mind.

I found it hard to articulate any words. Jay explained that Kahuna massages can leave people with extreme reactions from crying to feeling utterly excited and that it was important to rest afterwards. Then he said goodbye and disappeared into the spa to attend to his next guest.

I kept sitting for almost an hour in the tropical outdoor relaxation area staring at the delicate orange sheers that separated the chairs to offer some privacy. The golden afternoon sunlight wove its magic around the space. Something is going to change, my mind repeated over and over again. I savoured the lemongrass tea and the fresh fruits, which tasted so much better than the days before. I still felt like floating in this ocean of love. I didn't want to share with anyone what had happened. I wanted to keep it in my heart, cherishing that you could tell the most memorable story in a conversation without words.

CHILDHOOD MEMORIES I

My childhood home resembled a bee hive; always busy, business and private life interlaced. There was little separation; hardly a space to be alone.

Our house, in a small country town in the southwest of Germany, was three storeys high. The ground floor was divided into the bakery, convenience store, two storage rooms, one of which was also used as the office, and our kitchen, the hub of the house. On the first floor, which we shared with my paternal grandmother Lina and her second husband Alfons, there was another kitchen, three bedrooms and two living rooms. My paternal grandfather, Helmut, never returned from Russia, where he died from starvation in 1945 at the age of 36. According to my father, Alfons arrived around 1950, when my grandmother looked for a baker to restart the business after the war, as my father was still an apprentice and not ready to take it over. I always called Alfons 'uncle'. This is what I was told. I guess it was because he was eighteen years younger than my grandmother and didn't want to be called 'grandpa'.

We had only one bathroom and one toilet for five people. I had to enter my room either from the bathroom or my parents' bedroom, which became more and more of an issue the older I got. The top floor had four bedrooms and a bathroom which were never used, as they had been abandoned after the War. These rooms gradually deteriorated and became a place for storing all sorts of stuff. Over the years, my grandmother, who was a bit of a hoarder, kept accumulating anything and everything 'in the attic,' as we called the third floor, and it became more and more cluttered.

Some days I would go up there, open the door to one of the old bedrooms. Although the room had four windows, it was always dark because the outside blinds were down. I had to turn the light on. It was an interesting pendant, made of painted glass, an original from yesteryear. The room smelt stuffy but no one cared about opening the windows. I remember rummaging through old suitcases covered in dust; baskets and boxes hiding all sorts of stuff: old fabrics, sewing accessories, winter clothes, lamps, old hand bags, shoes, and umbrellas. One box contained a treasure trove full of fancy dresses, hats, gloves, belts, and bags that my parents would pull out once a year for the long Carnival weekend. Years later, when I was studying and living in Worms, I sometimes returned to one of the bedrooms in the abandoned attic on my home visits to work on my assignments. It was peaceful and quiet up there, and I enjoyed the view over the Rhine Plane.

Although we only had a few rooms that were ours, Mum always made them look nice and tidy. She had a beautiful sense of style, great taste and loved decorating. Quality was always more important than quantity. She used to say, 'if you buy something, invest in beautiful quality that will stand the test of time. You won't regret it.'

The ground floor was accessible from two sides: via the shop and the yard, which was closed off the street with a big timber gate. Apart from the customers in the shop, we usually didn't have unannounced visitors. Especially not when the gate was closed. The house resembled a castle, impregnable, with a high sandstone wall, which seemed to be insurmountable to me as a little child. I felt protected against unwanted intruders. As I grew older, I became more aware of what the thick wall was hiding from the outside world.

Everything seemed to happen in our kitchen: cooking, eating, baking, ironing, bookkeeping, studying. I did my homework at a pullout table under the bench. The same kitchen would be the place where my father was found dead more than 50 years later.

Our kitchen was a rectangular room with two windows facing the street just overlooking the sandstone wall and one facing the courtyard. An island bench divided the dining table with a corner bench from the cupboards on the opposite wall. For lunch, we would extend the table, as my grandmother and Alfons were eating with us during the week. Along the wall next to the door were more storage and overhead cupboards, the sink, and a gas cooking top. In the mornings, when I came down for breakfast, I would smell the freshly brewed coffee that my father had already made for my mother. Later on, my grandmother would start preparing lunch and the smell of fried schnitzels or a roast beef would permeate the ground floor. There was hardly a meal without meat. Every year in October, the kitchen was in a total mess when we used to pit tons of plums by hand for the many plum cakes my father would bake for the famous plum cake festival in our suburb. The hard work was rewarded with the delicious smell from the fresh cakes coming out of the oven. Plum cake is still one of my favourite cakes today.

My maternal grandmother Mina would come several days a week to tackle the ironing: I recall mountains of washing from underpants to shirts, pants, kitchen towels and my parents' work clothes; my father's stark white baker jackets with black and white chequered pants and my mother's white work aprons. These were the hardest pieces to iron, as the fabric was strong and stubborn. Grandma had to press hard with the small steam iron to make them look nice and the creases disappear. From time to time, steam clouds would appear above the ironing board and make funny noises. In no time, she used to iron men's shirts to perfection, and I always admired the end result. I would sit on a chair next to the bench and watch her. As she used to look after me quite often when I was little, I loved spending time with her and chatting away about all sorts of things. One day she told me a story from her life after the Second World War and how her ironing skills had saved her family. 'I hope you will never have to experience war,' she said. 'We often had not enough to eat for everyone. Only when I made a deal with the French soldiers to iron their shirts did I manage to get some bread and groceries for your mother and her brothers.'

Our house had been home to three generations like many others in the neighbourhood in the first decades of the 20th century: my father and his sister, their parents, and their maternal grandparents, Ludwig Wasem, who died in 1953, and Juliane Wasem, who died in May 1965, a week after I was born. The attic was home to the Zeitler family, a sister of my grandfather Helmut, her husband and their two boys. When my father married my mother in 1962, our house welcomed another resident. With me being born three years later, we were again three generations under one roof.

During my father's childhood years there was no heating in our house, and when the cold German winter hit, they used hot water bottles under their blankets to heat their beds at night. As young children, my father and his older sister Lilo slept in a room on the first floor facing the street, which would later become my grandmother's kitchen. Years later, as a teenager, and after the Zeitler family had moved out, my father occupied one of the four bedrooms upstairs overlooking the Rhine Plains. 'In winter, it was so cold that ice flowers decorated the windows,' he recalled. During my childhood years, we had gas heaters installed in the kitchen, the living rooms, the bathroom, and my bedroom. The rest of the big building, the staircase, the toilet, the entire second floor, was not heated and, therefore, ice-cold in winter. To protect the few heated rooms from the creeping cold, keeping the doors closed was paramount.

The yard, or Hof, was quite big and included several other buildings, some of which were attached to our house, others lined up opposite. It looked a bit like a patchwork quilt, as none of the buildings fitted with the other.

When my father was a young child, the cobblestoned yard was divided into a hog house with a large timber door with two panels opening separately, an adjacent dung heap, a couple of outdoor toilets, the only ones on the property until early 1950 when the first water toilet was installed, a wine press, and a chicken house. On the other side, there was a shed for storing shredded vines and briquettes to fire the oven in the kitchen. 'As a young boy, I went several times a day with my rucksack in the forest to collect fir cones we needed to ignite the fire in the kitchen and keep it burning,' my father explained. Next to the hearth in the kitchen, they had a big rectangular pan with a lid, which was filled with water and heated by a fire underneath.

The poverty of those years was extreme and hard to imagine. Apart from food, new clothing and shoes were difficult to buy. One day, my father and his friends played soccer on the cobblestone street in our suburb; when he kicked the ball, he accidentally hit the ground with his brand new shoes, and the sole ripped off. This incident led to a major drama with his mother, as new shoes were an absolute luxury those days and their lifespan had to be stretched as long as possible. The standard shoe had a thick timber sole – that would not bend a millimetre when walking – and must have been similar to today's clogs. To prevent the sole from wearing down, the parents would hammer ten to fifteen nails into the soles of the kid's shoes. As this material combination led to enormous noise levels when walking, small leather strips were added to cover the nails and reduce the noise.

After school, my father would mostly play outside, in the forest or the streets. As there was not enough food and the family bakery closed during the war, the kids used to walk along the streets of our suburb. 'Sometimes, we would find small pieces of bread stuck between the cobblestones.'

In those post-war years, the accessibility to food stayed paramount. The bakery was still closed, and bread was rationed to 300 grams per person per day. All families received food stamps for basic products such as bread, butter, sugar, and flour. 'We had to collect them, glue them onto newspaper pages and exchange them for food coupons at the mayor's office. Then, we would walk to Neustadt with a handcart to collect the groceries.' If the family needed vinegar, they would walk to a neighbouring suburb, where they collected the liquid in large barrels.

The families who had a garden were the lucky ones. Behind our house, a huge garden provided a source of fruit and vegetables. 'We had potatoes, cucumbers, salad, several vegetables, cherries, plums, and a Mirabelle tree,' my father recounted. As a child, I often played in this garden. With friends from the neighbourhood, we would climb the tree and serve ourselves from the branches abundant with ripe plums.

And that is how the yard looked when I grew up: adjacent to the house, next to the bakery, was our laundry with the washing machine and the dryer, a big double sink and an pissoir. Next to this building was an old shed where my parents stored paper and cardboard boxes from the shop to bring to the recycling station. Then there was a carport that we used for our second car apart from the transporter my father used to deliver his baked goods to other retail shops.

Opposite the main house, there was another carport with the original outside toilet or shit house, as the adults would call it in

Pfälzisch, our local dialect. The timber door had a heart carved out in the upper part, not only for decorative purposes I guess. Especially in summer, swarms of flies were buzzing inside the small cubicle. The smell was unbearable, especially if you lifted the lid to do your business. There was a timber bench seat with a round hole in the middle: dark, deep, and stinking. I used it occasionally when I was a child. I remember I had to climb on the bench seat, fighting the intense and penetrative smell. It made me nearly sick when I was in the cubicle. I wasn't there very often, but sometimes, when I played in the yard and needed to wee, the way upstairs to the toilet on the first floor was just too long. As we had only one flushing toilet inside the house, the outdoor toilet was still in use for some time. From time to time, there was a huge truck reversing in our yard to pump out the smelly content. Luckily, after my parents had built a second toilet on the ground floor, the outdoor toilet was emptied for the last time and officially 'closed'.

Adjacent to the carport was an old workshop, which used to be the pig's shelter in earlier years. It had one of those stable doors with two separate panels that you can open individually. I remember it as a storage room for my dad's tools, spare tyres for the cars, and my bike. Next to the workshop stood a large rectangle brick building with a massive timber sliding door. Inside, an old round wine press was centre stage. It looked like a big timber cylinder sitting on a round metal stand with a trough around the press.

Alfons owned several vineyards and had a small winemaking business on the side. Each year, in October, the grape harvest was a big event for the locals. The wineries were looking for casual harvest helpers. The women would cut the grapes and work their way up and down the long rows of vines. The men collected the grapes in big buckets, which they carried like rucksacks on their backs and unloaded the harvest into huge containers sitting on the trailer of the tractor. As soon as I was old enough, I wanted to help with the grape harvest. It usually was a fantastic day out when the sun was shining. However, autumns in Germany are not always sunny, and some days we had pouring rain that transformed the soil into a muddy and sticky mass that made walking along the vines a challenge. I remember one day my rubber boots got stuck in the mud, I stumbled and slipped out of one boot into the cold and wet soil. During the day, my foot turned into a stiff ice block in my boot. Rainy days combined with low temperatures definitely lowered the mood of the harvesters.

Back home, the wine press would come alive. The grapes were unloaded into the press and by applying pressure through a plate that was forced down onto the harvest with a handle, the juice would be extracted. It was always a spectacle to watch how the grapes were squashed in the press and how the juice was flowing out into the surrounding trough. I used to catch some with a small glass and enjoy the sweet drink. From the trough, the juice was directed into barrels where it would slowly transform into Riesling.

At the end of the yard, there was a small square lawn with a door leading to our garden and to the vast area of vineyards belonging to the suburb of Haardt. These were my playground during my childhood years. Together with other children from the neighbourhood, we would spend hours riding our bikes or roller skates in summer or go tobogganing in winter. We also loved exploring the small waterways between the vineyards, hidden amongst bushes and weeds; an adventure land to play hide and seek.

*****

Mum and I had a ritual, which we both cherished very much. Twice a year, when the new fashion for the upcoming summer or winter season had arrived in the shops, she would take an afternoon off and drive with me to Mannheim, a 30-minute drive from Neustadt, to browse the city's long shopping mall. We would visit lots of fashion boutiques, department stores, and shoe shops to find out what was 'en vogue' in the upcoming season. I loved trying on all sorts of beautiful clothes and shoes and admiring myself in the mirrors of the change rooms. We always chose at least one complete outfit for me: pants, jumper, shirt or blouse, jacket, and shoes – sometimes more than one pair. Mum always looked for good quality pieces and nice materials. Once we had finished our shopping adventure, we would find a lovely café and celebrate our fabulous finds with a coffee and a yummy piece of cake before we would return home.

Apart from retail therapy, Mannheim had more exciting things on offer. Mum was a member of the Theatergemeinde, a community of people who attended selected performances at the city's opera house every month.

When I was twelve, I got a new outfit for my very first visit to the opera, to see Haensel and Gretel. I felt like a grown-up wearing a beautiful long skirt in red, white and blue with a white blouse.

When we passed the massive glass doors to the spacious foyer of the theatre, huge chandeliers illuminated the space, making everything sparkle: sequined dresses, glamorous jewellery, handbags and shoes. People strolled around in small groups, a glass of champagne in their hands, chatting to each other, smiling, laughing, in anticipation of the upcoming performance. I felt like I was entering a fairy tale world of beauty, a world that made me happy.

Then, we heard a loud gong. 'We have to go up and find our seats,' Mum explained. The small groups of people dissolved and streamed towards the huge staircases on one side of the foyer leading to the large hall with the orchestra pit. Slowly, one big stream of people climbed up the stairs, women holding their long dresses, cautious not to step on them while walking.

When we had finally found our seats, Mum asked me: 'Can you smell the Theaterluft?' There was this special smell coming from the stage and requisites – a bit stuffy, dusty, somehow mysterious. I sniffed the air trying to grasp this unknown odour. I looked around in awe, soaking in this grand atmosphere; my eyes noticed all the details around me: the velvet upholstery on the seats, forming long rows in a semicircle around the orchestra, the boxes on the sides stacked diagonally behind each other, the many lights along the ceiling, big spotlights that illuminated the stage. People were busy finding their seats and making themselves comfortable. Muffled chatter mixed with the cacophony of sounds coming from the orchestra who tuned their instruments. There was a sense of community, of belonging to the same tribe, a comforting feeling to which I surrendered in anticipation of the performance.

'Mum, what's that black box at the edge of the stage?' I wondered after observing the scene for a while.

'That's the place for the prompter,' Mum explained.

'What's a prompter?'

'A lady who helps the artists on the stage in case they forget their words.'

'Oh, and what are all the lights for?' I wanted to know next. Not waiting for my mother's answer I bombarded her with more questions about all the new things that I discovered.

'Who is sitting in these boxes on the sides? Are they reserved for special people? How many people are in the orchestra? What instruments do they play?'

I will never forget this first visit to the opera, although there were many more in the following years. Each time I went to the theatre later in my life, I tried to smell the Theaterluft and only now do I understand that these outings were one of my mother's way to escape her daily grind in our uneducated household.

MY TRUE HOME

"When we return to the right here and now with the energy of mindfulness, we will be able to establish our true home in the present moment."

Thich Nhat Hanh, At Home in the World

*****

'I've had enough of this!' The cutlery jumped up from the plate when I hit my right fist on the table. 'You know what? I am moving out, so you don't have to worry about my opinion,' I screamed at my husband while I pushed back my chair and got up noticing my sons' surprised faces. I grabbed my sandals, handbag, and car keys and left the house.

Suppressed emotions had erupted from deep within me. 'You can't talk to boys like that' was my husband's last sentence that made me spit out boiling lava like a volcano. Uncomfortable conversations were not familiar in our household. That day it was about helping more with household duties. We had shortly discussed it before dinner but not yet determined exactly who would do what and when.

However, instead of just telling them what I expected, I wanted to discuss with them that as a family we would need to work together as a team to make things happen and also help each other out with the chores, such as setting the table, tidying up, taking out the rubbish, washing and ironing, for example. It was also important to me to make my teenage son aware that his often rude way of talking to me was not the way women wanted to be talked to.

It was the end of January 2017, and since our return from the retreat, the voice inside telling me to leave my marriage had become louder and louder. When I pulled out of the driveway that evening, I decided to go for a walk along Manly beach to process the thoughts that tumbled through my mind. I ended up at the secluded lookout at Shelley Beach with vast views over the ocean and Sydney's Northern Beaches.

I leant on the railing and took a few deep breaths soaking in the salty ocean spray. Luckily, the only bench in that small spot was empty. In the next hour, I listened to podcasts about mindful living from Thich Nhat Hanh, a Vietnamese Buddhist monk. What he was talking about resonated so much with me that I became quieter and quieter. His teaching to live in the present moment and to make each moment the most beautiful moment in your life were like balm for my soul. To practise love and compassion for yourself first in order to treat others with kindness, love and compassion was something that I wanted to prioritise from now on.

In the past four weeks, I had reflected on many things and for the first time managed to express my feelings to another person, my coach Karina. We only had met shortly at a networking event a couple of months earlier and she was the only person that came to my mind when I went through all my contacts to find someone to talk to about my experiences and emotions. The reality was that I felt empty and indifferent in my marriage. There was respect and gratitude, but no more love for the man with whom I had been living together for 23 years.

When I felt calmer, I left the lookout and headed back to the beach for a walking meditation, which I had read about in one of Thich Nhat Hanh's books. After three hours, I returned home. That night, I made the decision not to engage any longer in those disrespectful conversations with my husband and sons.

The next morning, I escaped to my 7:30am yoga class. Exactly three weeks after my memorable Kahuna massage, Keenan, one of the master facilitators in the studio, started his class with the introduction that in our yoga practice we involve three parts of ourselves: the body, the mind, and the spirit. With our physical body we progress through the asanas, concentrating on our breath to keep the mind focussed on the practice. To involve our spirit can be the hardest part. Keenan encouraged us to focus on the mantra 'I am...' without filling in the blank, without labelling ourselves.

Then, towards the end of the 90-minute class, he concluded that we all have this notion of inner peace within us, a place of love, a place that is hard to describe with words; but we would know when we have found it. During the final resting pose, I found myself floating in the same space that Jay had shown me three weeks before: a place of love and compassion, of inner freedom and happiness. At the end of the class, Keenan encouraged us to take this notion of peace with us throughout our day. Hours later I could still feel being uplifted and grounded at the same time. I smiled at random people in the supermarket and received surprised looks in return.

I reflected on Keenan's words and noticed how much yoga had changed me over the past six years. The practice had helped me step out of my comfort zone more than once, which led to meeting new people, finding new job opportunities and tackling challenging situations.

I started reading books about Buddhist teachings and philosophy. First, I devoured At Home in the World by Thich Nhat Hanh. In his collection of autobiographical stories, I found a couple of stories that were eye-openers for me, as I tried to understand the spiritual experience I had encountered.

The first story was called The Hermit and The Well where Thich Nhat Hanh recounted a childhood experience. His schoolteacher told his class one day that on top of a mountain in North Vietnam there lived a hermit – a monk who sat quietly day and night to become peaceful like Buddha. Thich Nhat Hanh was very excited as he had never met a hermit before. The next day, the class set off for the trip to the mountain. When they had climbed to the top, they still had not met the hermit, and the young Thich Nhat Hanh was very disappointed. He kept climbing further and further up until he found a natural well, a big pool surrounded by rocks. As he was very thirsty from the strenuous climb, he knelt down and drank some of the refreshing water from his hands.

He wrote: "The water tasted so good. I had never tasted anything as good as the water. I felt completely satisfied; I didn't need or want anything at all, even the desire to meet the hermit was gone. I had the feeling that I had met the hermit. I imagined that perhaps the hermit had transformed himself into the well."

Even as an adult, he could remember this profound, spiritual experience. "It was many years ago that I climbed that mountain. But the image of the well and the quiet, peaceful sound of the dripping water are still alive inside me. You too may have met your hermit. Maybe as a rock, a tree, a star, or a beautiful sunset."

When I read this story, I realised that I had met my hermit during my Kahuna massage. This treatment had changed my life. I felt more grounded, mindful and reconnected with myself; at the same time, uplifted and excited about the year ahead. I would never forget the energy of inner peace, love and compassion that streamed through my body after my treatment.

CHILDHOOD MEMORIES II

As a child, I spent quite some time at my grandmother's place and have a distant memory of the room layout. My mother's childhood home was a rectangular-shaped apartment on the first floor of a three-storey building with rooms on either side of a long narrow hallway. My grandmother's bedroom and the living room were on the right side facing the street. Opposite her bedroom, my mother's older brother, Klaus, had his room. Mum slept separated from the main apartment. Maybe because she was the only girl, born in 1941, with four brothers who had to share their rooms eventually. My uncles were born in 1939 (Klaus), 1944 (Günter), 1947 (Robert), and 1950 (Helmut).

I never met my grandfather Carl August Disson, who was born in 1894 and passed away in December 1963, two years before I was born. From my uncles I learned, he died of cirrhosis of the liver, a horrible death, as the result of drinking too much Riesling.

As in my father's family house, the kitchen was the centre of the home. A big table in the middle of the room took pride of place. The original sink was huge and made of sandstone which made it always look dirty. Later on, Uncle Günter gave it a makeover by tiling it. The apartment had neither a bathroom nor a toilet. I remember standing in the kitchen as a young girl being washed in front of the sink. My uncles told me that they also had a zinc bathtub stored vertically in a recessed corner of the kitchen. When they grew older, they used to walk to an indoor swimming pool in Neustadt to have a shower. The toilet was located in a small room outside the apartment and, like the one in my father's family home, a round hole in a timber seat. The container underneath was connected to a large sewage pipe running vertically from the top to the ground floor. According to my uncles, nobody wanted to be there for too long, especially not if someone on the floor above was doing their business at the same time.

Underneath the house was a large cellar – cold, damp, and stuffy. It became one of the most important rooms during the war. 'When we heard air raid warnings, we all ran downstairs,' Uncle Klaus explained. 'Our mother would clench Heidi under one arm, Günter under the other, and I would hold her apron and run behind them down the stairs. We would sit in darkness on mattresses inside a table turned upside down, waiting until it was safe to return upstairs. Our mother, her friend Katharina from the neighbourhood, and Frau Schaaf, an 80-year old woman living in our house looked after us; three old women always dressed in black. We had to stay in the darkness until the bombing was over.'

My mother never spoke about her childhood memories during the war. She was probably too young to remember, but this will always remain a secret, as, unfortunately, I never attempted to find out how she experienced those years.

Luckily, the family survived the air raids and had never been in direct danger from bombing. However, as Klaus recalled, playing in the streets was risky too, as telephone lines and power wires had been ripped down and were hanging loosely from their poles. 'We never knew which cable was the power line,' he explained. Nevertheless, the streets, the garden, and the forest were their playgrounds for most of the time. When inside, my uncles praised my mother's skills playing Mühle (nine men's morris) and Halma. 'Heidi was hard to defeat in these strategic games,' Robert revealed in 2015 when I was in Germany to research my family history.

As a young child, I learned to play Halma with Grandma when I stayed with her overnight. Later, the board game moved to our house, where I kept playing it with my mother. It became one of my favourite games; I loved the bright coloured board and touching the little timber figures that had a smooth, almost velvety texture. When I looked for old photographs of my parents in our living room cupboard, I found the vintage game. Touching the old worn box and feeling the smooth timber stones brought back lovely childhood memories.

'We never had to starve, but the food was scarce,' Klaus confirmed the stories that my father had told me. 'Sweets or bananas were a special treat when they could get hold of them. In the post-war years, the women in the village would go Hamstern – walking long distances to the countryside and offering domestic services to whoever could give them something to eat in return. As Klaus recalled, my great grandmother Wilhelmine Marx – she had the same first name as my grandmother – used to be a very skilled seamstress and would sew for the farmers in exchange for potatoes and vegetables. One day, she came home with a sausage, about ten centimetres long. 'Our mother divided the sausage between all of us, but our father would get the biggest piece. That's how it always was.'

The French soldiers, who occupied Neustadt after the war, not only would rummage through the homes of the locals and take everything they wanted, but also confiscated the produce of the farmers. They collected all the potatoes, for example, and transported them on big trucks through the village. As the potatoes were piled up in the back of the trucks, the drivers sometimes lost some of their load. My grandmother who was pregnant at that time would follow the truck in the hope of catching something to cook for her children. One day, she and some other women were caught by the soldiers and had to return what they had picked up from the street. As if this was not enough, all of the 'thieves' were imprisoned for one day; except for my grandmother, who was lucky and escaped the punishment because she was pregnant.

My mother not only had to support my grandmother in raising her younger brothers but also help with household duties; she would have to scrub the socks of her brothers with her hands until her knuckles were bleeding. Aunt Rosa, the wife of mum's youngest brother Helmut, remembered conversations with Mum complaining about the hard work at home. Being the only girl, she had to do all these chores and didn't receive any special treatment in return.

When Mum had finished school, she was expected to learn 'something' and had to start an apprenticeship with a local coffee roaster in the village. Her parents expected her to marry and leave the house as soon as possible. 'Every night, she would come home crying,' Klaus told me. She couldn't stand the smell of the roasted beans hanging in her clothes and hair after hours in this shop. 'I don't want to do this any longer,' she begged for sympathy from her parents. But my grandfather, who was already in his mid-60s, ignored her. So she took her destiny in her own hands, successfully applied for an apprenticeship with a big insurance company and managed to leave her hated job eventually. Dressed in beautiful outfits, she would go to work in a nice office environment in the city.

Her positive spirit and enthusiasm stood out for everyone I interviewed. As Klaus confirmed, my mother came across as a very optimistic and good-humoured person, always a smile on her lips. And she was worth two boys, as he told me proudly. Once, when they were playing outside, and older boys bothered them, my mother didn't run away, but rather attacked the boys with horse manure that she found on the street. The boys, utterly surprised by this unexpected attack from a younger girl, took to their heels much to the delight of Klaus. As the oldest siblings, they seemed to have a special relationship, which, one day, led him to brand her. According to his story, he only wanted to scare her. Mum was kneeling in front of the sofa in the living room reading a book. He took the poker, not thinking how hot it was, approached his unsuspecting sister from behind and pressed the hot metal against my mother's neck. Only when she started to scream like crazy, he became aware of how painful it must have been. My mother had a lifelong scar from her brother's attack in the living room.

However, this incident didn't seem to affect their relationship. Mum was always eager to help her older brother. When she worked as an apprentice for the insurance company, she had connections to a textile trader, who would supply her with the latest fashion in ties. For two Marks she would sell the ties to her brother and receive a small commission from the supplier. Klaus regularly showed off his newest addition to his wardrobe at the next night out. "I would wear the fashionable ties with a white  shirt for the next dance party and impress all the girls," Klaus reminisced about his outings with a smile on his face.

Mum was always famous for a grand entrance. In the late 1950s, she had met my father at one of the local dance parties. When they started dating, my father would drive up with his white and red Porsche cabriolet on Sunday mornings, waiting for my mother, who would gracefully slide into the car. She would wear a chequered skirt, with a petticoat underneath, a large belt emphasising her waist and a white V-neck blouse, sleeves rolled up to the elbows. 'She behaved like a diva,' Klaus described the scene. Off they went, much to the delight of the entire neighbourhood, who were watching the spectacle from their windows.

In 1962 my mother married my father and moved out of her family home on Hauptstraße 16 to my father's place on Hauptstraße 164, a kilometre away at the other end of the village. She gave up her job in the insurance company and started working in my paternal grandmother's Tante Emma Laden, a small convenience store where the local community would be served from behind the counter.

As a young child I remember standing between the long dark timber counter and a massive storage unit with shelves and drawers, with big timber knobs along the wall, displaying all the groceries for sale. Goods were presented in large glass containers with lids, lined up on the shelves; the same glass containers you find nowadays in antique and vintage shops. Nothing was sold in packets; everything was scooped from sacks, drawers, or glass jars. Big scales to weigh groceries, fruit and vegetables sat on the counter. There were a number of weights next to the scales, ordered in a row from small to large. To me they looked like a row of toys, neatly arranged and something to play with.

In 1965, the year I was born, the retail landscape in Germany changed with over 1,000 supermarkets already registered in the country. They started to replace the traditional convenience stores, who now started to fear for their existence in times of progress and change.

*****

As a young teenager, I became more and more aware of what was going on in our family home. My father hardly talked to his mother and random conversations about mundane things would turn into heated arguments.

My mother also told me that my grandmother had forced my father to become a baker, although he never wanted it and was truly passionate about cars and playing the trumpet when he was young. Like many other kids who grew up during the war, my father left school after eight years and started his apprenticeship in a bakery in a nearby suburb at the age of fifteen. "As a baker, you will always have something to eat" was his mother's argument in support of following the footsteps of his father and grandfather. Follow your passion was out of question in those days and not a message he heard when growing up. 'What I would have loved to do is an apprenticeship as a mechanic and then study mechanical engineering.' My father revealed his dream career path at his 80th birthday in 2015.

Over the years, I noticed how unhappy he had become because he worked in a profession he didn't enjoy. As a consequence, he never had an interest in developing the business and making it more profitable. His relationship with his mother was indifferent and cold; they hardly spoke or spent time with each other.

My father's helplessness in dealing with his mother became a latent crisis in our daily life. The whole situation became more aggravated over time as she constantly interfered with our private lives, my father's, my mother's and eventually mine as well. She would enter any room without knocking on the door.

I also learned that my grandmother, who owned another property in the village, had bequeathed our house to my father's sister and her family. She had declared in her will that my father would inherit our family home after her death, and that Alfons was allowed to live in our house until his death should she pass before him.

One day, I saw my mother counting money and putting it to the side after she had closed the daily cash accounts. When I asked her what this sum was for, she replied that we had to pay a monthly rent to my grandmother because we took over her business and lived in her house. There were many things that seemed completely unfair to me, and I wondered why no one ever said anything or tried to discuss it with her.

I felt sorry for my father because of the way his mother had raised him without love or compassion and that he didn't have the courage to speak up and to stand his own ground. But to see my mother trapped in our household made my heart ache. For years and years, she seemed to be the mediator between all parties, and everyone spoke extremely highly of her, including the people in our village. She always tried to make the best of every situation, helped where she could and was the go-to person for everyone. At the same time, she neglected her needs and mostly put herself last. And I could feel deep within me how much she suffered. What made it worse was the fact that I couldn't help her.

When my grandmother started interfering with my life as a teenager, I disliked her more and more, loathed her even. I couldn't stand it when she just walked into my room. I didn't want to bring any of my high school friends home, as I was ashamed of my grandmother's behaviour and our family situation. Most of my friends lived in big and beautiful private homes, quiet, pristine, secluded in residential areas without the noise, the dirt and the rubbish from a bakery and a shop. Our ground floor, the entrance, the kitchen and the shop were always covered in breadcrumbs and flour traces that my father and Alfons would spread all over the place when walking around. Every day we had to sweep the floor several times.

Our days were structured around the rhythm of my parents' work hours. During the week, my father would get up at 4 am to start baking. On Saturday mornings, even earlier. Mum would get up at 6 am to open the shop at 7:30 am. Over lunch, the shop was closed between 12:30 and 3 pm, when it re-opened until 6:30 pm.

We used to have casual workers helping out in the shop. Apart from running the shop, Mum was in charge of the daily book keeping, the weekly orders, unpacking the deliveries and filling the shelves, which often needed to be done after hours or on a Sunday, her only day off.

I longed for Saturday afternoons when finally the house was quiet and clean. At 1 pm the shop would close and the entire ground floor including the bakery, storerooms, the shop, our yard and the pavement around the property would be cleaned. Once finished, the weekend started with the very German ritual of having coffee and cake mid afternoon.

The older I became, the bigger my desire grew to leave our house and move into a space of my own no matter how small it was.

***

At high school, I started with Latin as first foreign language in Year 5, followed by English in Year 7, and French in Year 9. In my first year of high school, I met Ulli and Suse, who became best friends and are still 40 years later.

I kept studying Latin for nine years and mostly enjoyed it; however, our skills were extremely challenged in Year 9 and 10 when we had Dr. Friedrich Burkhardt as our Latin teacher. I still see him in his grey suit, white shirt, black tie, and black bag entering the classroom. His black hair shiny with gel combed backwards. He was one of the old school: strict, correct, not tolerating any nonsense. He was not very tall but radiated an unassailable authority. The entire class was scared of his appearance because we never knew what would happen on the day. He usually pointed out one of the students to read out loud the passage we had to translate for homework. He then would ask you to translate it into German and finally bombard you with additional questions regarding the Latin grammar. The first minutes of his lessons were always nerve-wracking. We all had our eyes fixed on our tables, avoiding eye contact with our teacher, and hoped that we would be spared this time from homework revision. At the same time, we all knew that it would be our turn one day.

This was the time when Suse, Ulli, and I decided to take on the challenge and improve our Latin language skills through private tuition with Suse's uncle, who was a lawyer and very proficient in Latin. He offered us weekly private lessons on a Saturday afternoon from 4 to 5 pm. We decided to commit to this voluntary extra lesson on a weekly basis, including homework, although it interfered slightly with our Saturday evening program: the dance school.

As most teenagers, we were enrolled in our local dance school in Neustadt to learn the basics of ballroom and Latin dancing. Here my love for ballroom dancing was born. I remember that I always hoped the dance teacher would pick me to demonstrate the moves, as he was the only one who could lead properly and knew what he was doing. Most of the boys our age seemed to be embarrassed with the whole dancing thing and quite awkward when leading the girls around the floor. On Saturday nights, the dance school would organise a social dancing event from 5 to 10 pm. As our parents would pick us up at 10 pm sharp, and this disco night was the only place for teenagers under the age of eighteen to go out, we didn't want to miss a minute of it. The place was usually packed, hot, sweaty, and terribly loud, but we didn't want to be somewhere else on Saturday nights. We kept going there until we turned eighteen and were finally allowed to visit 'real' night clubs.

Unfortunately, I didn't pursue ballroom dancing further.

CURIOSITY AND COURAGE

"We tend to live life in ignorance of the fact that everything is moving in cycles. And with that, we tend to think that we are separate from the cycles that everything is moving in. If we take a step back, we can see the bigger picture."

The Cycles We Live in, College of Universal Medicine Blog

*****

I arrived half an hour early to the first evening of the six-week workshop Understanding Menstruation & Menopause, which I had come across through a recommendation from a therapist at the retreat. Listening to my body, I had booked it shortly after my return to Sydney. I was curious to say the least. According to the brochure, this workshop was for women, who are interested "to deeply connect to the true purpose and gift of their cycles."

The sparsely decorated Lindfield Community Hall was set up with a circle of twelve chairs and a large screen on the back wall. There was only one other woman and Katie, the facilitator, when I arrived. I chose a chair a sat down. We didn't talk a lot while we were waiting for the other participants to arrive. The circle of chairs filled over the next 30 minutes, and we were ten women altogether when Katie welcomed us officially to the six-week workshop.

She introduced the course as a forum for women, who are interested in deeply connecting with their body and cycles. She encouraged us to share our experiences with menstruation and menopause and informed us that we would learn to understand our cycles better and to listen to our bodies in our every-day life. Only by listening to our bodies would we have the opportunity to take a more active role in improving our overall wellbeing.

The first evening evolved around the two cycles menstruation and menopause. Some of the women shared their stories of their time as teenagers when they had their first bleeding. It quickly became apparent that in a lot of cases there was hardly any communication around menstruation, and young women were often left alone with their thoughts, fears, and feelings. Menstruation was dealt as something you don't talk about and women were encouraged not to make too much fuss about it.

We had to fill out a questionnaire about our experience with menstruation and menopause, and I found it even hard to remember at what age I had my first bleeding. Memory is malleable, and any attempts to dig out some snippets of conversation I might have had with my mother were in vain. I never spoke with my grandmother about this topic. I made notes of the menopausal symptoms I was experiencing from irregular bleeding to hot flushes, irritations, and bad sleep patterns.

Time went by quickly, and on my way home I kept thinking about the diverse stories I had heard that night.

*****

The main topic of the second evening was to debunk the myths around menopause. We spoke about phrases associated with women entering midlife. Katie read from an article published by the College of Universal Medicine, which listed statements, such as "being over the hill or on the downhill side, no longer attractive or desirable, invisible to men, and over 50."

Then, she read out a long list of beliefs around menopause, which seemed dominate the public opinion: Women entering menopause "will no longer enjoy a full sex-life, shrivel up and age rapidly, gain weight around the middle, lose bladder control more frequently, no longer hold the same value as a woman of child-bearing years, no longer have anything valuable to contribute to society beyond baby-sitting their grandchildren."

A list of doom and gloom, which made me think that it was no wonder that many women did choose not to share their emotions and feelings with their family or friends. After we had listened to these myths, I started contemplating about the stories the other women had shared and tried to remember with whom I had spoken about this new phase of my life. Apart from Karina, I had mentioned my hot flushes and sleeping problems to a few female friends and my husband.

Next, we started talking about our relationships to our teenage children. I shared a story about how my communication with my 15-year-old son had improved when I used some of the tools Karina had explained to me.

'As the parenting cycle comes to a close, you can start sharing more with your son as a woman, rather than as a mother,' Katie confirmed.

At the end of the session, Katie asked us to explore the many pictures we live to as a woman and how this way of living separates us from who we truly are.

This was the second time on that day that I heard the word 'exploration'. I had spoken about it with my life coach in the morning. The act of exploration requires a combination of curiosity and courage, values that are both very close to my heart. Curiosity and courage brought me to Australia nine years ago. Curiosity and courage made this book a reality. Curiosity and courage opened the door to my innermost self and set free my Goddess. Curiosity and courage finally helped me to speak up and live my truth. I didn't know yet that curiosity and courage would make me discover ballroom dancing nine months later.

FARAWAY LANDS

My parents only could afford to go on a holiday once a year. The bakery and shop would close for three weeks, and we would either drive or fly to a European destination. This summer holiday was my highlight of the year because we finally could spend time with each other as a family without unwanted intruders. As a young child, I remember holidays in Switzerland, Spain, and France. Over the years, we travelled several times to our neighbouring country France because Mum learned French at an evening school and wanted to practise her language skills.

I guess these early trips planted the seed for my continuous desire to travel. My curiosity to explore other countries, to find out more about their culture and history made me pack my bags and leave trusted ground. Wandering through the streets of a foreign city and becoming the observer of the trivial, the unexceptional, the commodities of life; soaking in the places, the atmosphere, the people – that is what made travelling so interesting. At the same time, I never lost sight of my domestic roots.

By the time I finished high school, I had decided to study business administration at a technical college which required an apprenticeship or an eight-months internship as a prerequisite to enrol. As I was keen to improve my French, I applied for an internship in a hotel in France.

One day, a letter from the Hotel Frantel Toulon landed in our letterbox. I still remember that I was sitting next to the bench in our kitchen, staring at the envelope after I had found it in the daily mail pile. Holding my breath, I ripped it open, unfolded the letter and quickly scanned it. I read that they would be happy to accommodate me at their hotel for my internship from September 1984 to April 1985. I jumped up from my chair, ran out of the kitchen to find Mum to tell her the exciting news.

On the 30th August 1984, I boarded a train from Frankfurt to Marseille where I would have to change trains to Toulon, my final destination. I travelled overnight and arrived at 6:30 am the next morning at Marseille Central Station. 'The night in the train was horrible' I recorded in my diary. I had hardly slept not knowing if I was more scared or excited about my adventure. Travelling alone still gave me a funny feeling in my stomach, although I had just come back from a six-week trip to Spain. This time, however, I knew I was going to be away from home much longer.

Marseille is not only the second largest city in France after Paris, it is also a major hub for the French speed train TGV. The moment I stepped onto the platform of Marseille central station, the reality struck me: I was alone in this big city over a thousand kilometres away from home. I took a deep breath and tried to suppress the slight panic that was building up in my body. What would I find when I'd arrived at the hotel? How would I cope with work and having to converse in French all the time? Around me, a few workers mingled with early passengers finding their way on the platforms. The city was slowly waking up. Not having any answers to all the questions that were flashing through my mind I decided to have a coffee and a croissant in a nearby café – partly to fight my loneliness, partly to fill my stomach that had started rumbling – before continuing my journey in a regional train travelling along the coast to my final destination. The hotel where I would spend the next eight months, was situated below Mont Faron, a 584-metre high mountain overlooking the city.

When I finally arrived, I introduced myself at the reception: 'Bonjour, je m'appelle Bettina. Je suis la stagiaire de l'Allemagne.' I had to concentrate hard to hide my nervousness and talk casually. My heart was beating frantically, and I hoped no one could hear it.

'Hello and welcome,' replied the man at the reception, looking a bit bewildered as if trying to think what he should do with me on a Saturday morning. When I showed him my letter from the hotel director, he told me that none of the management team were available and that I could speak to them on Monday morning. Luckily, he knew which room I was going to stay in and accompanied me to the second floor. He then handed me the key and went back downstairs to resume his work.

There I stood, in a narrow L-shaped room with a single bed, a wardrobe, a sideboard, and a small table with a couple of oversized chairs. The furniture was worn and looked dated. Opposite the entrance door, there was a tiny ensuite bathroom. The only window looked out to a rocky landscape on the side of the hotel and was set back underneath the floor on top. As a result, I didn't have any views nor a lot of light. The room was the final straw to make me feel even more lonely. However, there was no alternative at this stage, and I unpacked my suitcase.

I felt so lonely and lost in this place, where no one seemed to have waited for my arrival on this Saturday morning. I went down to the reception and decided to call home. I disappeared into the telephone booth near the reception desk – somehow relieved that no one could hear my conversation with mum. When she answered the phone, I couldn't stop my tears. I was telling her that I had arrived safely, but that I felt so alone and didn't know what to do. I wanted to take the next train back home. I could hear that mum was also swallowing her tears, but then she said something to me that I have never forgotten.

'You can't come home now. You just arrived. It will all be good once you start working.'

And so I stayed. I spent the following eight months in different departments of the hotel and became fluent in French. At the end of my internship, I even supported the Sales Manager in organising an exhibition in Mannheim, the city I knew so well from my theatre visits and shopping trips.

In April 1985, after returning to Germany, I started studying business administration with a focus on hospitality and tourism in Worms (a city on the Rhine River 80 km north of Neustadt).

I believed that this career path would give me the best chances to find a well-paid job. I kept ignoring my heart and my interest in design and interior architecture and aimed at a position in public relations.

Three years later, I found a place for an internship in a small editorial office in Mainz, the capital of the state of Rhineland Palatinate and moved 20 kilometres further North along the Rhine. These three years working with a team of two journalists sparked my interest in the writing and publishing industry and laid the foundation for my professional career of 16 years in public relations.

*****

I didn't know a lot about Mexico when I started working at the international PR agency Fleishman-Hillard in Frankfurt in 1991. However, this changed quickly, as one of my clients was the Mexican Tourism Office. The more I read and learned about the country, the more intrigued I became. I was eager to practise my Spanish language skills.

In November 1992, my boyfriend and I arrived in Cancún, the tourist Mecca on the Yucatán Peninsula bordering the Caribbean Sea. Armed with a road map and a dictionary to back up my basic knowledge of the Spanish language, we started to explore the Yucatán Peninsula with its world famous Mayan cities Tulúm and Chichén Itzá, Mérida, one of the many colourful colonial cities of the country, and finally the Pacific coast. My work for the Mexican Tourism Office included media relations for the boutique hotel Villa del Sol, located at Playa La Ropa in a postcard-like setting in Zihuatanejo Bay at the Pacific Ocean, 240 kilometres north-west of Acapulco. The owner and manager, a German entrepreneur, had invited us to stay five days in his hotel, which was one of the highlights of this trip.

***

The year 1994 was an interesting one in many respects. I was single again and would often spend the weekend with Ann-Christin, a colleague from the PR agency who had become a very good friend and who lived in Frankfurt-Sachsenhausen. I also embarked on a couple of exciting trips to Asia, found new friends, and met Martin, my future husband.

Ann-Christin and I would often read the Journal Frankfurt, a very popular city magazine, featuring everything that was going on in Frankfurt. The section that interested us most was the Lonely-Hearts ads. After several trial and errors, one day I came across an ad that instantly made me smile: "Australian, without belly and beard, is looking for female..." I decided to find out who this guy was and replied with a letter to the magazine. Not long after the phone rang.

'Hi, my name is Martin, you answered my ad in the Journal Frankfurt.'

I noticed his broken German and thought that he must be that funny Australian 'without belly and beard'. I found myself being investigated about what I did for work, what my hobbies were, how many languages I spoke, and where I currently lived. After answering his questions for about twenty minutes, I wondered why I was giving all this information to a complete stranger on the phone!

'You are very curious,' I said in an attempt to stop him somehow, 'and want to know lots of things in the first phone conversation.'

'That's my job,' he replied briefly, 'to find out things about people.'

He then explained that he worked as a managing consultant for an international consulting business that had transferred him from Sydney via London to Frankfurt. After chatting away for a while, we then decided to meet for dinner at a Thai Restaurant in Wiesbaden. As it turned out, although working in Frankfurt, Martin had rented an apartment in a private home in Wiesbaden opposite the city of Mainz where I lived on the other side of the Rhine.

A few days later, we met for dinner. I learned that he grew up in the Adelaide Hills in South Australia, where his German parents had immigrated in the 1950s. He had lost his father at the age of twelve and left home to join the Australian Navy at the age of 15. Twelve years later, he started a career in the corporate world as a management consultant in Sydney. He always wanted to learn more about his parent's country of birth and applied for a position in the Frankfurt office. His employer eventually transferred him to the Frankfurt office.

Over dinner, he explained that German was his first language when he grew up and that he had to go to a Saturday school to practise his mother tongue. The longer the evening, the more we felt at ease with each other. I remembered Ann-Christin's words, encouraging me to bring the Aussie to her birthday party the next day if he turned out to be a nice guy.

The day after I sat in Martin's blue BMW and we drove along the Autobahn to Frankfurt. Soon we were all squeezed into her tiny place, having a good time. From this day on, we started going out and got married seven years later, on the 21 September 2001, when I was pregnant with our first son.

Apart from meeting my future husband, 1994 was a very exciting year, as I travelled to Asia for the first time, explored Hong Kong and Indonesia, discovered Buddhism, learned to eat with chop sticks, and made new friends along the way.

Ann-Christin and I worked as a team and we looked for additional clients in the hospitality and tourism industry. As I always wanted to work for an airline, I started cold-calling their Frankfurt offices. It so happened that the marketing manager of the Hong Kong airline Cathay Pacific Airways was looking for a new agency and we were invited to pitch for their account. We won the business and embarked on an exciting couple of years.

Until 1994, I had never travelled to Asia. Working for Cathay Pacific sparked my desire to explore this region. I made several memorable trips to Hong Kong and Shenzhen in Southern China as well as an adventurous backpacker trip to Indonesia.

Working for Cathay Pacific Airways was one of the highlights of my early career in public relations. Apart from the privilege of accompanying groups of German journalists to Hong Kong, the marketing manager became a friend. We found out that he had relatives living in Neustadt-Haardt opposite my mother's family home and that he had studied at the same technical college in Worms. After I had left Fleishman-Hillard in 1995 to continue my career at a PR agency in Wiesbaden, we stayed in touch and became friends. I was devastated when I learned in 2001 that he had been diagnosed with terminal cancer.

CHOICES

"Disregard means putting other people before yourself."

Jean Gamble, Psychotherapist

*****

It was the first week in April, and I enjoyed the freedom of being alone at home for the first time in 15 years. No schedules, meal times or afternoon driving duties; freedom to do what I wanted and when I wanted. I soaked in every minute of each day to fill up my energy tank for the time when my life would be once again dictated by my role in the family.

My husband had taken Max and our visitors to the Northern Territory to visit Uluru before they made their way to Queensland where Valentin and I would meet them for our Easter holidays. I had contemplated of going away for a couple of days but then listened to my body and decided to stay at home.

Every week, I was looking forward to Thursday night when we would meet again for the workshop. In the third session, we discussed the topic of disregarding our bodies. Katie had invited Jean Gamble, a psychotherapist, to present on disregard and self-sabotaging patterns. It promised to be an interesting evening.

'Disregard means putting other people before yourself,' Jean explained. She also mentioned that, depending on your personality, disregard expresses differently. It can be as simple as not going to the bathroom if you need to or not having a rest when you are tired. She named addiction to alcohol, drugs or nicotine as more severe expressions of living in disregard.

We had a lively discussion about how we disregard our body and how this manifests every day. We agreed that as women we were champions in putting other people first and not taking care of our needs. Neglecting our bodies resulted in a lack of self-love and self-worth. Many women shared stories from their marriage and how the dynamics had changed after they had decided to listen to their body and to stand up for what they believed was best for them. Jean reminded us to always stay true to ourselves and not deviate from our values and beliefs.

While the discussion went on, I made a mental list of all the situations where I had disregarded my body in the past fifteen years. Snippets of conversations, images of situations appeared in front of my eyes as the list grew longer and longer.

As a mother, I did what most mothers do; I always put my children first, sometimes to the extent of total exhaustion. I remembered how I always thought, 'I can't get sick, I have to keep going' to juggle everything. My whole life centred around the boys' needs, and I never complained about it.

There seemed never enough time to look after myself, to indulge in a bath as often as I would have liked to, or to book a massage. Instead of lying down to rest in the few hours the boys slept when they were little, I squeezed in my duties around the house. During the time I breast-fed the boys, I hardly went out to socialise as the constant sleep deprivation left me depleted. I always wanted to start painting and it took me years until I finally made the first attempt during a family holiday. However, I never took art classes, as I couldn't find the time to fit them in with my part-time job, parenting duties and household chores. Although I have always loved reading, I didn't make the time for it during those first years with my children. It was the way it was, and I never questioned it. I just kept going with what everyone expected me to do.

And so the years passed, the boys grew up and became less dependent from me. I started to get a glimpse what this new found freedom could look like in the future. The one thing, however, I had not considered were the changes in my body followed by a never before experienced clarity of my mind when I entered peri-menopause.

With this clarity came the realisation that I was still disregarding my body, especially in the relationship with my husband. We had no culture of communicating with each other about the stuff that really mattered. Since we had moved to Australia, I had become more and more unhappy in our marriage. I kept neglecting my emotional needs, I swallowed frustration and anger when I should have spoken up.

When I thought about how often I had kept my mouth shut in all the years we lived together instead of seeking the conversation with my husband, it was mind-blowing. Why was it so hard to talk to the man I had known for so long? The more I looked at my life from a bird's perspective, the more I realised that I had grown up in an environment where no one was very good at talking to each other. What was even worse was that we were raising our boys in the same environment. This realisation was a wake-up call, and I was determined to change the conversation culture in our household; a mammoth task in a family that mainly concentrated on unimportant small talk. The work with Karina gave me the courage to seek uncomfortable conversations and to trust my feelings rather than my thoughts. And I knew that I would have to seek more of those uncomfortable conversations in the future.

At the same time, I felt empowered by my feminine wisdom, which I had finally learned to trust. To discover my innermost self, had triggered the desire to reconnect with my body, to acknowledge it more and to nurture it as often as I could. This self-care included my daily yoga practice or resting when I was tired, even if it was only for fifteen minutes in the middle of the day. I also prioritised daily time for reading, writing, and self-care. When I saw that Mother's Day and my birthday fell on the same weekend in May, I decided to return to the retreat and have another Kahuna massage. But first, I had to face our upcoming Easter holidays in Noosa.

ABOUT DYING

In 1998, my maternal grandmother Mina lived in an aged care facility. At one of my last visits, we chatted over a cup of coffee. She was always interested to hear what was going on in my life. Then she said with a sad voice: 'You know, I can't stand it any longer to see Heidi suffering.'

At the beginning of the year, Mum's condition had worsened again. 'I have to go to the hospital,' she told me. About ten years before, she had been diagnosed with breast cancer. After initial surgery, the cancer stopped spreading and she was granted eight years of treatment-free living. Unfortunately, in 1996, it struck again; this time with vengeance, spreading through her bones.

I felt a lump in my throat when I heard the bad news, but swallowed it and reassured her that I would make sure to come and visit her regularly. She moved into a room in the radiology ward at the Mannheim University Hospital, which specialises in cancer treatment.

The next couple of months were excruciating. Apart from the mental stress and the permanent anticipation of hearing more bad news, I drove the 80 kilometres from Wiesbaden to Mannheim after work as often as I could. It was a scary visit. The radiology ward was separated from the other buildings; I had to walk through long corridors until I would finally reach the big double door with the massive red and black warning sign 'Radioactive Radiation'. Every time I arrived there, I had to force myself to open this door. The atmosphere was cold and eerie. I hardly saw any patients, nurses, or other visitors. This was a ward where the severe cases were dealt with, cancer patients with little or no hope of recovering. It was heart-wrenching to know that Mum was in one of those rooms, captured, waiting for her daily treatments. Not knowing when they would allow her to go home.

One afternoon, I had a work appointment in Mannheim, I dashed in the hospital before driving home. Mum asked me to wash her hair, as she couldn't do this any longer. We were sitting on her bed afterwards, when she looked at me and said: 'You know, I am not afraid of dying. I am more afraid of what I still have to bear up with.' I gave her a big hug and swallowed hard to hold back my tears.

Despite her illness, she still had the desire to help others. One day, I accompanied her and the professor who treated her to a classroom full of medical students. A few days before, he had asked her if she was willing to share her story as a cancer patient with his students. She was sitting next to the professor in the auditorium with a room full of young people looking at her. She openly talked about her illness to complete strangers, sharing how cancer had influenced her life. After her talk, the students asked questions and then said good-bye with standing ovations. I felt so proud of her. When she learned that she was going to die but that her organs were not affected by the disease, she decided to become an organ donor; one of the many ways she contributed to other people's lives.

After seven weeks in the hospital and no communication from the doctors how long Mum would need to stay, I decided to ask for an appointment with the professor, who was in charge of Mum's treatment. Together with my father, we were sitting in the professor's light-filled office in the hospital. The sun was shining and created a friendly atmosphere in the room; an atmosphere to make us feel good, to embellish the news we were going to hear. The professor, dressed formally in a white doctor's coat, offered us a seat in front of his desk.

'Let's not beat about the bush,' I started the conversation with a dry mouth and cold hands. 'What is going on with my mother? She has been here for seven weeks, and no one has given us any information when she will be discharged. I want to know the truth.'

'Look,' his voice softened, 'we are like the fire brigade trying to extinguish a blaze, but we can't keep up. Every time we are successful in one spot, the flames take over another area. It's hopeless.'

What followed was silence; a silence that paralysed me, only interrupted by the ticking of the wall clock. I tried to digest this final message. The brutal clarity I had asked for. I swallowed and breathed, keeping myself together. Hopeless. The word still echoed in my head when I thanked him for his honesty. What else was there to say? We shook hands, said good-bye and left. The spring sun was still shining, hitting the windows with no curtains, warming up the long corridor we followed back towards the radiology ward. We remained silent. My head was spinning with thoughts, uncontrollable, messy. What now? How long? How is she going to cope at home? What will my father do? How will it be without her? Too many questions without answers.

In March, not long after our conversation with the professor, they finally released her. Mum was very fragile, and the drive home seemed to be like a horror ride for her. I saw her terrified face in the rear mirror; she was sitting in the back of the car as if she had never driven on the Autobahn at 120 km/h before, clinging to the seat in front of her. After almost three months in her tiny, cocoon-like hospital room, the real world seemed to wash over her like a tsunami.

To cope with daily life at home was challenging. She spent most of the time in my room, where she could escape the busyness of the house. We arranged an in-home care service from the Red Cross. Nurses would come on a regular basis to look after her. My father suddenly found himself in charge of everything, the business, the household, looking after my mother – a situation he was not used to and that was too much for him. Luckily, three of my aunts lived in Neustadt and came regularly to help out or just chat to Mum to distract her from her illness.

But there was more to come. In May, only a few weeks after Mum's hospital release, I answered a phone call from Aunt Rosa. I was at home in our apartment in Wiesbaden when she conveyed the sad news about my grandmother: 'Mina has passed away last night.'

At her funeral shortly afterwards, Mum could hardly stand on her feet as the cancer kept eating through her bones. She couldn't attend the ceremony in the chapel at the cemetery either; she was brought in the car just in time to see the coffin being placed in the open grave. Leaning on a stick, she burst into tears while she said farewell to her mother. It was heart-wrenching. I couldn't suppress the thought of how much more time Mum would be given in this world.

*****

21st July 1998, 6 am. It would be another hot summer day. I raced down the Autobahn from Wiesbaden to the Neustadt, talking on the phone with one of my colleagues at the PR agency. I told her that I would not come to work, as the hospital had called last night to inform me that Mum's condition had further deteriorated and that I should come rather sooner than later.

7 pm. I was sitting in one of those uncomfortable plastic chairs in Mum's hospital room, at the edge, leaning forward to hold her hand. She looked exhausted. Her eyes were closed. Above her head, the morphine pump steadily filled her body with the drug. My father and two of my mother's brothers, Klaus and Robert, were also present.

I had just returned from our home, where I had escaped for something to eat after spending the entire day in this sterile room. It was as if she had waited for me to return. The evening sun painted the outside world and parts of the room in a warm, golden colour. It was very quiet, as if some fairy had cast a spell upon us. Nobody moved or said anything; everyone seemed to wait for the inevitable to happen. After a while, Mum opened her eyes and looked at me for the last time. I held her hand and smiled. I lacked the strength for more. Then, she closed her eyes and stopped breathing. I put my head next to hers on the cushion, giving her a last hug. All I thought was: Thank you, God, for relieving her from this suffering.

Uncle Klaus broke the silence: 'We must inform the nurse,' and left the room. I was still sitting at Mum's side holding her hand. A few minutes later, the doctor rushed in, feeling her pulse and telling us what we already knew: Mum had passed away. He shook my father's hand, who, burst into tears – something I had never experienced in thirty-three years. 'She was a wonderful person,' I heard the doctor say. He came over to me, shook my hand as well and expressed his condolences. He was a friendly guy, and I had met him several times throughout the previous ten years. We all hugged each other, somehow relieved that a long fight had finally come to an end. No one was crying after my father had composed himself again. After a while, two nurses on duty entered the room and asked us to leave. They needed to get everything ready to take her to the basement of the hospital where they kept the corpses until they were picked up by the undertaker to be prepared for the funeral. It was Mum's wish to be cremated and buried in our family grave in Haardt next to her mother.

We left the room. Like a robot I dialled Martin's number. When he picked up the phone, I heard myself say: 'It's me. My mother has just passed away.' I told him that I was going to stay with my father overnight. I was still not crying.

Later on, in the evening, I sat on the edge of my bed in our family home, staring in front of me, trying to comprehend what had happened in the past twenty-four hours.

The night before, after a hot summer day, Martin and I had decided to drive out of Wiesbaden to have dinner at a lovely restaurant in the forest. In summer, it was a one of our favourite places, as the air was fresh and much cooler than in the city. In the middle of our dinner, the phone rang. It was the hospital asking me to come as my mother's condition had deteriorated. I listened and then heard myself saying that I would come the next morning. In hindsight, it was crazy, as I had risked not seeing her again before she passed away. But, at that moment, my body refused to go. I would leave the next morning. I am a morning person, and mornings have always been my preferred time of the day to get things done – anything really.

Mum was gone. Sitting on the edge of my bed in my family home I felt alone, overwhelmed by the thoughts that streamed into my mind. And then, finally, my eyes filled with tears and flowed over, a stream of salt running down my cheeks. How would it be without Mum? How would it feel not to be able to tell her what happened in the past week? Not to have my mother and my best friend any longer?

All of a sudden, my father opened the door to my bedroom, looking at me crying. We both didn't say anything, and after a few seconds, he closed the door again and left me alone. I felt like an orphan, as the relationship with my father was never particularly affectionate. Even after we had both lost the most important person in our life, we didn't move closer together.

Mum's funeral was a big event in our little suburb. A lot of people came to say goodbye and express their condolences. We kept the shoebox full of sympathy cards for many years. The chapel in the beautiful cemetery in Haardt was bursting with mourners, some of them had to stand outside in the hot August sun. I was sitting in the front row next to my father, my uncles and aunts. I can still see random people appearing on my right side, stopping in front of the coffin, sobbing, and holding handkerchiefs to dry their tears. Some of them came to us, shook our hands and murmured some words of solace. Others just nodded in our direction. The funeral was both mourning and celebration of her life. The fact that we lost her at this young age, just 57, was hard to understand. What would she have wanted to tell us? To leave us with? Not just dad, me, her brothers and sisters-in-law, but the huge crowd of friends, customers and acquaintances, who gathered there that day. 'Life goes on,' she might have said, 'so make the most out of it.' The eulogy was spoken by a female Protestant priest, a lady from our neighbourhood. I can't remember, though, what exactly she said. Then, the coffin was rolled outside and carefully loaded into a car that brought her to the crematorium.

As Mum had not made a will and my father kept living in our house, most of her things stayed there. We never officially came together to sort out her belongings. In one way, I was glad that we didn't do it, as dividing up her things would have enforced the ultimateness of her absence. I slipped back into my daily life in Wiesbaden, where I was not surrounded by her presence, into my role as public relations consultant that was demanding and offered enough distraction not to be reminded of her all the time. In the following months, I often found myself thinking, 'I have to call Mum to ask her about this,' my phone in my hands, ready to dial her number, only to realise in the same instant that she would not answer the phone and that I would never hear her voice again.

Over time, I gathered a few things from our family home that reminded me of my treasured time with her: her favourite pearl necklace and bracelet, a collection of scarves, a beaded clutch she used to take to the opera, a special edition of Nobel Prize winning books from 1901 to 1970, a notebook with handwritten recipes, one of her children's books with her name written inside, a tiny purse for a small handbag, one of her favourite winter coats.

I never spoke with my father about his feelings after Mum had passed away.

In the weeks after the funeral, I started reflecting on my mother's life. I remembered one day when she had told me that after her apprenticeship she had not been courageous enough to follow her heart. Her employer, an insurance company, had offered her a position in their headquarters in Munich. She would have had to leave my father and move to a big city, 300 kilometres away. 'I wish I would have gone,' she said to me once. 'This might have changed my life completely.' But she stayed. Trapped in our uneducated family home, suppressing her emotions for many years. I tried to imagine my mother's career and life in Munich. Who would she have met and married finally? What lifestyle had she missed? In which house would I have grown up? How would our life have unfolded?

With many unanswered questions, I returned to Wiesbaden and succumbed to my daily life, distracting myself with work. In the following ten years, I climbed the career ladder in the PR agency, got married, gave birth to two boys, renovated a house, moved, looked after my sons while working part-time and kept living the life I was supposed to live on the side of my husband. However, my inner voice didn't go quiet. I had been reflecting on my life for a while and was questioning my career in public relations. Would I do this until retirement? I loved my job, but there was always the longing to work more creatively; to do something different. Stuck in old habits, however, I kept ignoring the voice in my head and kept doing what I was doing.

Until one day in summer 2007, when my husband told me that he had been offered a job in Sydney. Moving to Australia had always been looming at the horizon. Suddenly, the move had become very real. While I digested the news, I felt deep inside me that this was a sign from the universe; a sign I had been waiting for since I had lost the two most important women in my life. It was my chance to explore something different, an opportunity to change and to start a new chapter of my life. And so I jumped in with both feet.

NOOSA

"Our deepest fear is not that we are inadequate. Our deepest fear is that we are powerful beyond measure."

Marianne Williamson, A Return to Love

*****

The week in Noosa was an interesting one, an eye-opener, really.

In the previous four days, which I had spent alone at home, I had tasted the sweetness of total freedom. To be by myself provided the opportunity to listen to my heart and let my body dictate my daily life. I went to yoga every morning, ate when I felt hungry, worked until I was finished without interruption; enjoyed our living room listening to music without the TV killing any kind of conversation.

I cherished the solitude more than anything else, and my mind travelled back in time when I was single and lived in a tiny studio apartment in Germany. If I was honest with myself, this solitude was what I was craving every day since our return from the retreat almost four months ago, and I felt a slight resistance in my gut when I had to pick up my 12-year-old from his school camp on Friday afternoon. Only to pack and get ready for our flight the next morning to the Sunshine coast.

I was also a bit nervous about how I would interact with my husband after my coaching session a couple of days before. We had done very deep emotional work where I had cut the cords with him and cleared the past. Afterwards, my coach explained to me that I would now have the chance to reconnect with him from a different place; a place of feminine wisdom; a place of simplicity; a place of feeling rather than analysing. I had decided to approach this week with curiosity and openness to what was going to happen.

However, I had not anticipated that the first thing I learned would hit me right at my core. I was flabbergasted when I heard that I would be alone with Valentin on his birthday because my husband had booked a trip to the Great Barrier Reef with our visitors, including Max.

Hendrik, one of Max's childhood friends from Germany, had stayed with us for a school term. To finish off Hendrik's trip to Australia, Martin had been travelling with Max, Hendrik and his father the previous week to Uluru and the Northern Territory and had planned to fly to the Whitsunday Islands to crown the Australian experience with a visit to the Great Barrier Reef.

But life does not always work out as planned. Cyclone Debbie had pummelled the Queensland coast and wreaked havoc on the Whitsundays. As a consequence, all flights were cancelled. As the original plan had collapsed, Martin decided to take our car and drive up the coast to Gladstone to catch a boat from there to the Reef. However, Gladstone also had cancelled all trips due to the cyclone's devastation. As plan B had failed as well, the next idea was to book a flight from Hervey Bay to Lady Elliot Island where they would spend the whole day snorkelling, walking on the island and admiring the Reef from glass bottom boats.

'How could you book this trip on Valentin's birthday?' I asked in disbelief. 'He was so much looking forward to it and couldn't wait to get here for his special day.'

I felt that he had again prioritised other people over the family. The entertainment of our guests was more important than celebrating with his son on his birthday, which we could have incorporated into the program for our visitors. We had repeatedly spoken about the fact that Valentin's special day would fall into the holiday week. The topic was chewed over the next couple of days but due to high season nothing could be changed.

I tried to stay calm in the face of our visitors. However, my heart was heavy, I felt disappointed and disrespected. And with each day that passed, I bowed to the inevitable that I drifted further away from my husband like a boat that is carried away by the waves from the safe harbour.

*****

'Hey, Dude, how is your birthday going so far?'

Max, a bit awkward but with compassion in his voice, looked down to his younger brother.

'Great!' Valentin replied, smiling. His mouth was circled with a ring of chocolate chip ice cream. They both had just devoured a monstrous double-scoop cone from one of the local ice cream shops. Max, although 15, didn't look much different to his younger sibling as far as the face-painting was concerned.

The three of us stood at Hastings Street, the main tourist strip at Noosa Heads. The boys and I had had breakfast together in our holiday villa, as Valentin couldn't wait to finally unpack his iPhone, which we had promised to give him for his 12th birthday. Of course, he could hardly eat anything so exciting was his new mobile device. With Max on his side, he swiped and typed through the procedure to set up the phone.

'I really like just being with Max and you, Mum,' Valentin expressed his feelings on his special day.

Afterwards, we headed down to the beach, which was only a 15-min walk from the accommodation. We had a good time together, and I felt the bond between us strengthening every minute since I had made the conscious decision to talk from my heart rather than my head to my sons.

The day before, we had been out for a walk. 'Mum, I'm very sad that they forgot me,' Valentin confessed. I felt a fist clenching my heart and gave him a big hug.

'I know, Sweetheart, it's not fair but we can't change it now.'

'Mum, I could stay back and spend the day with you and Valentin,' Max suddenly suggested.

'What do you think, Dude?' He addressed his younger brother.

'Oh, yes, that would be great!' Valentin exclaimed, and his face brightened up.

Later on, Max informed his father with such determination that Martin called the tour operator to cancel his seat in the plane. So it came that the three of us spent Valentin's birthday together.

I felt that the trip to Noosa had strengthened the bond between me and my sons in the most beautiful way. On the other hand, I became aware that I was becoming more and more estranged from my husband. After my coaching session the week before, I felt even more distant from him. During the next few days, the feeling grew and I wished more than once that I had stayed at home by myself. We hardly spoke with each other, and if we had conversations they were awkward and superficial. I avoided spending time with him alone and felt uncomfortable sleeping in the same bed.

One night, while the full moon illuminated the clear night sky, I woke up and felt like I was suffocating. I found it difficult to breathe. I escaped to the outdoor terrace. It was brightly lit by the moon, who shone in all its glory surrounded by twinkling stars. I sat there for a while, soaking in the fresh air, and sipping my hot tea. Then, I started to meditate. I prayed to God that I would have the strength to have the inevitable conversation with my husband. I knew now that I had to break the pattern of non-communication and suppressed emotions, otherwise I would end up like my mother.

According to an article on Psychology Today, research found "that suppressed anger can be a precursor to the development of cancer, and also a factor in its progression after diagnosis."

Especially anger that is not overtly expressed but instead swallowed and bottled up.

I had also read that many women with breast cancer have a tendency to hide their emotions behind a stoic face and stay in relationships where they give much more than they receive.

It finally dawned on me that I was living the life of my mother. She never had the courage to speak up and to express her feelings. She kept disregarding the signals of her body for many years. At 42, she was diagnosed with breast cancer and had a double mastectomy. She kept going with her life, always strong and hiding her true feelings until, ten years later, the cancer reappeared in her bones and spread through her body making itself heard with a louder voice. It was the beginning of the end, and Mum passed away at the age of 57.

Only now that I found myself in midlife, did I realise that I had followed the pattern of my mother's behaviour, I had disregarded my body and the signals it had sent all those years. I had arrived at a point where I couldn't keep pretending.

No wonder that this clarity was reinforced during full moon, a phase in the lunar cycle that supports cleansing and reflection as I had recently learned in the workshop Menstruation & Menopause. I was intrigued by what our body can tell us if we only listen.

As my body longed for another Kahuna massage, I had booked an appointment in Noosa. I was curious how this massage would be different to the one at the retreat, or if it was different at all. Would I again be bathed in this ocean of love and compassion? Would every Kahuna experience be as profound as the one I had with Jay?

The address I received in my confirmation email was in one of Noosaville's quiet residential areas away from the tourist strips where the practitioner had transformed a small space near the entrance of his home into a massage treatment room. Scott greeted me with a broad smile on his face:

'Great that you're a bit early,' he said.

He invited me to the small room, which was just big enough to fit the massage bed in the middle, a small chair and a sideboard. He asked me to fill out one-page questionnaire about my general health and asked me, like Jay had done, if I was happy to have my chest and abdomen included as well.

He then left the room and asked me to get ready. In contrast to Jay's lengthy introduction into the Kahuna massage style, Scott didn't explain it at all, maybe because I had told him that I was familiar with it. When he came back he only mentioned that he would not talk to me during the treatment. I closed my eyes and succumbed to the magic of his hands and forearms. It was a deeply relaxing and nurturing treatment with many movements I remembered from Jay's massage. Scott, who had been trained at the same institute as Jay, was similarly skilled. However, I didn't connect with him on the same deep emotional and spiritual level.

When I drove home, I was in good spirits as I now had the clarity that my massage with Jay had had something miraculous about it and that he would always be a very special person in my life. "Miracles themselves are not to be consciously directed. They occur as involuntary effects of a loving personality, an invisible force that emanates from someone whose conscious intention is to give and receive love," I read later in the week in A Return to Love by Marianne Williamson. Four months after meeting Jay, I could still see him in front of me with his right hand on his chest explaining "that Kahuna comes from the heart."

On the flight home, sitting amidst my teenage sons, I reflected on this week in Noosa, which had illuminated two things: one, the most important men in my life right now were my sons; and, two, the one relationship that I wanted to nurture and cultivate in the future more than anything else was the one with myself.

DECISIONS

'Mum, when are we going to move to Australia?' Max, my six-year-old son was looking at me; his dark brown eyes firmly directed to my face – challenging me once again. It was early 2008, and we had just come home from kindergarten.

His words hit me like a smack in my face. Frozen in action, questions flashed through my mind: 'How could he have found out? Had he overheard one of our conversations, or found one of the books about Australia that I had bought?

Max kept staring at me, sensing that he was onto something. I had to make a decision, quickly. I pulled myself together, took a deep breath and told him that, yes, he was right, we were going to move to his Dad's country of birth at the end of June 2008.

'Ok,' he replied, somehow relieved, and rather content that he had proved himself right. 'How long is June away?'

I explained that we would leave after he had finished his school year and that he would start year one in the German International School Sydney at the end of July. To make it a sweeter treat I added that he would go to a brand new school as the German School had just moved to new premises in Terrey Hills, a suburb inland from Sydney's Northern Beaches.

We had kept our plans to move to Australia to ourselves as long as possible, while we focused on getting all our ducks in a row for the big move. The past months had been busy with organising my visa. Then we had applied for Australian passports for the boys, who had automatically had become Australian citizens by descent when they were born in Germany.

In spring 2008, we started telling our parents and closest relatives about our decision. The reactions were a mixed bag of excitement, astonishment, and sadness. My father, as usual, didn't show a lot of emotions and accepted my decision without further discussions. I can't remember what exactly he said when I conveyed the news but something like: 'If that's what you have decided to do, go for it.' Over the past ten years, we had only seen us twice or three times a year, and the greater distance would not bring that much change in the future.

My to-do list of things that had to be organised before our move became longer and longer and was a welcome distraction not to think too much about what I would leave behind. We started selling our investment properties and our family home. I went through all our private documents informing insurances, investment funds, and government bodies about our emigration overseas.

Then, the day had come to pack up our household. A team of four men arrived at 7 am and started wrapping and packing in several rooms at the same time. At 3 pm, the heavy metal doors of our massive 40-foot container closed with a bang. Two hundred and seventy items of furniture and boxes, all our belongings, including my red sofa, had slowly but steadily been swallowed by this massive storage facility in the past eight hours. Every box labeled, meticulously registered in the loading documents. Ready to go on a long journey to the other side of the world. We had no idea that it would take much longer than the anticipated six weeks.

The moment the truck was out of sight, I turned around and looked at our house, an empty shell, which had lost its soul. It was not our home any longer. We had sold it a few weeks ago to a neighbour across the road. The impact of our decision to leave Germany hit me like a tsunami hits the shore. There was nothing to hold on anymore. I felt rootless and disconnected from this place, which had been our shelter for the past five years. To sell our property was one of the hardest things for me. I had put so much love into decorating it and making it our family home. It was the little things that had made my heart sing every time I entered the front door: the mirror we had purchased in South-

Africa which embellished the entrance hall; the boys' first works of art from preschool sticky-taped on the kitchen door; a bunch of flowers on the bench. All this was gone, the house abandoned.

We made our way to the City Hotel near Wiesbaden Central Station, which became our shelter for the next three days. I felt estranged from the city I had called home for the past thirteen years. All our belongings fitted in four suitcases. We had sold our cars and were walking or travelling in buses or taxis to get around. I realised that we were, all of a sudden, foreigners in Wiesbaden.

We spent our last days in 'good old Germany' visiting friends, eating out in our favourite restaurants and cafés, and soaking in as many impressions as possible; grateful for the years we had lived in this city, to which we would stay connected forever through our memories of many happy events: our first date, our marriage, the birth of our children. Our boys, Max, six, and Valentin, three, enjoyed their last day with our nanny. It was hard to say good-bye, and we both had tears in our eyes when she handed the boys over to us for the last time. 'I have a small present for each of you,' she said pulling a couple of photo albums out of her bag. Each with a collection of images of the boys' favourite after school activities, such as going on bus rides with her, visiting a horse stable or eating pasta with tomato sauce in her apartment.

On our last day in Wiesbaden, I answered a call from Singapore Airlines; the staff member from reservations asked when our return flight was booked.

'There is no return flight,' I answered with a lump in my throat. 'We are going to move to Australia.'

'Well, then, good luck!' he wished us well before he hung up.

CONVERSATIONS

"Work with what you've got, and more will be revealed."

Jaime Dickson, Senior Minister Seaforth Anglican Church

*****

Several weeks had passed since I had been to church. On the last Sunday in April, I hoped that the church community would be a kind of safety net to prevent me from falling deeper into a dark chasm.

I had finally taken all my courage and expressed my feelings to my husband after breakfast. As expected he didn't blow up or lose his composure. However, he seemed not to want to hear what I was saying.

'We should do more things together,' he kept insisting.

'I need some time and space for myself to reconnect with my body and to sort out what I want to do with my life in the future,' I made another attempt to explain the transformation I was going through.

I told him how I had finally realised that I had been living my mother's life for a long time, namely suppressing my emotions for years and avoiding uncomfortable conversations about the things that matter. I felt that the lack of communication in our relationship and family had played a major role in the development of our marriage. I also expressed my worries that we raised our sons in the same environment and that I was determined to break this cycle before it was too late.

We kept talking for over an hour, and I felt more and more miserable with a fist clenching my heart. The immense relief I had envisaged after this difficult conversation didn't come. At some point, the situation became unbearable, and I stopped the excruciating discussion. However, there was no solution and my heart felt sad. How many of those conversations would I still have to initiate?

The day passed in a fog with me not being able to concentrate on much and I escaped to church in the afternoon. I was greeted as usual with many friendly smiles and 'How are you, good to see you again' exclamations. As soon as I had taken my seat in the second row, Jaime, the minister, greeted me effusively:

'Hi Bettina, how are you? It's great to see you again! When you were here with your husband for one of our church dinners a while ago, I could finally make the connection between you and Martin. I have seen him over the years at the bus stop in the mornings and we sometimes chatted. It was such a surprise to see you both together on that night.'

The clump in my stomach tightened. I muttered that I felt quite exhausted after having visitors for three months in our house. I wanted to reveal myself to this sincere and warm-hearted man, who had received me with open arms in his community. But this was not the right time with the service about to start in five minutes time. So I remained silent.

'Well, I hope our church will be a sanctuary for you today,' he replied and moved on to greet the people next to me.

That Sunday, Jaime started a new sermon series about Jesus' parables. He pointed out how difficult it often was for his disciples to understand him and that only the ones who were excellent listeners were able to reveal the underlying meaning of his stories and to tune in to Jesus' message. He compared this act of tuning in with the old radios where one had to turn a button very carefully to find the right frequency to get a clear sound and hear the program. He also mentioned that it can be hard for the ones who are tuned in to God's message to convince family and friends to try and tune in to the right frequency. He encouraged the congregation with the words 'work with what you've got, and more will be revealed.' Words that resonated very much with me.

I had another sleepless night feeling more and more uncomfortable in our marital bed. Deep inside me I knew what to do.

The next morning, I moved into our guest room, where I created my own little retreat for the time being. I pulled out some clothing, T-shirts, jumpers, yoga gear, and some of my personal things from my bedside table: my books, a notebook and a pen. I moved my cosmetics and towels from our ensuite to the main bathroom, which I would now share with the boys.

Thinking about them made me feel worse. How would they react when they saw my stuff in the guest room? What would I say to them? I decided to talk to them in the afternoon when they returned from school.

When I approached Max, he was already immersed in his computer game, his ears covered with headphones.

'Max, I need to talk to you. Could you please stop for a minute?'

'What do you want?' His eyes still fixed on the game, he hardly turned his head.

'Could you please stop for a moment, I have something to tell you,' I made the next attempt.

'Yes, I heard it, what is it?' he replied slightly impatiently and uncovered one of his ears.

'No, you have to stop for a moment, I need you to look and listen to me. It's hard enough for me,' I raised my voice and stayed adamant.

He finally uncovered his ears and turned around.

'I have moved into the guest room today and will use the main bathroom with you and Valentin for the time being. Just in case you wonder why all my stuff is in there. I'm not getting along with your Dad very well at the moment and need some time and space for myself to sort out what I want to do in the future.'

'Hm, ok,' Max seemed not at all surprised and focussed his attention back on his computer game.

That was it. I left the family room relieved that I had managed the first hurdle. Now, I would need to talk to Valentin when he returned from soccer later that day.

I approached him after dinner on his way into the bathroom.

'Valentin, I need to talk to you quickly before you hop in the shower,' I started.

He stopped in the door and looked at me with curiosity.

'In case you are wondering why all my stuff is in your bathroom, I moved into the guest room for the time being and will share the bathroom with you.'

'Yes, I saw that,' he replied.

I repeated what I had told Max a couple of hours earlier and, to my surprise, got exactly the same reaction.

'Ok, Mum,' was all he said and went into the bathroom to get ready for bed. Mentally exhausted, I fell into the guest room bed and had another sleepless night.

THE LAND DOWN UNDER

We arrived in Adelaide on a chilly winter morning in June 2008. The boys stayed with my mother-in-law, while we flew to Sydney to organise the most important things to start our new life: a car, a fridge and some rental furniture for my husband's apartment in Mosman, which we had renovated for our arrival. A neighbour lent us a bed, a table and two chairs for the time being.

After a couple of days, we realised that our plan to move in with two little boys was not going to work. The apartment was too small and had only a balcony and tiny front garden belonging to our upstairs dwelling. So we decided to sell it and find a place to rent for a few months.

As my husband had to start working the next day, I faced the challenge of finding a house in the next five days. This turned out to be more difficult than I had anticipated. Firstly, most landlords didn't want to lease their properties for less than one year, and secondly, I had unexpected difficulties in understanding my conversation partners. Although my English was pretty good, I had not anticipated the Australian accent! I was used to my husband's way of speaking and was expecting everybody else to speak like him.

After several fruitless attempts to find a rental property in Mosman, I dialled my husband's number.

'What do we do now? I can't find anything appropriate in the area!'

'Ok, let's look at the adjacent suburbs, 'Clontarf and Seaforth.'

'Where is that?'

'Just over the Spit Bridge.'

Clontarf, Seaforth, Spit Bridge – who had come up with these strange names for suburbs and a bridge? Were people spitting from that bridge into the harbour? I couldn't imagine that a bridge would be called Spuckbrücke in Germany. But, again, there was no time for philosophical reflections about the naming of Australian landmarks in those first days. I started searching for houses in Clontarf and Seaforth, without any idea where these places were. I obviously needed a rapid course in local geography and noted this on my mental to-do-list.

"Property to rent for six months" was the first search result showing up in Clontarf. I couldn't believe my eyes; a five-bedroom house with swimming pool. After quickly clicking through the images, I had already decided that this was going to be the one. I called the real estate agent and arranged for inspection the following Saturday. We visited the house and decided on the spot to rent it.

However, there was another hurdle to overcome. The owner of the property lived overseas and we had to wait for his approval hoping that it would come through on time because our sons, who we had left in Adelaide with their Grandma, would fly to Sydney the following Thursday. In the end, it all went to plan and we could move in our new home four days later, just on time before the boys arrived.

The next trip led us to the furniture rental company. We chose beds, a dining table and six chairs, a sofa and a coffee table for three months, which turned out to be a better deal than just booking for a few weeks; a wise decision as we would find out later.

The first few weeks in our new home were challenging. The boys were on holidays, as the German school had just closed for four weeks. My husband was at work, and I tried to settle in our new home, entertain my sons and get to know the area we had moved to. I knew that if wanted to get out of the house, I needed to jump in the deep end and start driving our new BMW. I will never forget my first trip to Warringah Mall, a big shopping centre on Sydney's Northern Beaches. With my hands gripping the steering wheel, my eyes glued to the windscreen, and my brain trying to focus on the cars in front, staying on the left side, the traffic lights on the other side of the crossing, and following the signs to the mall, I was challenged in many ways. The 15-minute drive seemed like an hour. Once I arrived, I took the first possible entrance to the carpark and luckily found my car again later. After this first driving experience, I became more courageous and hit the roads every day. A couple of weeks later, I got used to driving on the other side of the road and was surprised how quickly it became second nature to me.

We slowly settled in. After the first month in the 'Yellow House' as the boys called it because of the yellow exterior paint colour, the children started at the German International School in Terrey Hills. To meet other Germans was consoling, as we all tried to find our way in this big city in a foreign country so different from the place we came from. 'We are all in the same boat' was an often-heard phrase in those first weeks.

However, the language barriers increased. Sydneysiders seemed to hardly open their mouth when speaking – to not let the flies in, I learned later. They mumbled and used words I had never heard before. Kindy, cossie, esky, barbie, hubby, brekkie, brolly, footy – What English was this? I had read about this peculiar Australian – or should I say Aussie – habit in my emigration guide, but it was a different thing to hear the words in real life and, of course, to try and work out what they meant. I was not aware of any other English-speaking nation using so many abbreviations in their language. After studying English for ten years and practising it almost daily during my professional career, I started to question whether we had been sufficiently prepared to cope with the specificities of the English language around the world.

After a while, I got used to all sorts of strange conversations – strange to me because they would never happen in Germany. On one of my first visits to the supermarket, for example, the lady at the cash register smiled at me while starting to pack my bags:

'Hi, how are ya today?'

I looked up from my trolley wondering if she was talking to me. As she kept grinning at me, I quickly answered: 'Thanks, I'm fine.' After handing over another bag to me, she continued the conversation:

'Anything special planned for the rest of the afternoon?'

Slightly bewildered, I was trying to think what to answer now. Did this person really want to hear what I was going to do that afternoon? While she continued scanning and packing my grocery – oblivious to the fact that I had not answered her yet – I didn't want to appear rude, and replied:

'Nothing much,' hoping that this would be the end of this unexpected interrogation in the supermarket. She seemed to be happy with my answer and finished off my purchase.

I thanked her for packing the bags – this was a luxury that I didn't know from Germany – and heard her saying:

'Have a nice afternoon, darl!' Although I had no idea why she now called me 'darl' and didn't know what that meant, I couldn't help but grin while I pushed my trolley towards the exit. That was the first time in my life that supermarket employees had asked about my day and seemed to enjoy a conversation with their customers. Later that day I asked my husband what 'darl' meant and learned that it was the abbreviation for 'darling'. I couldn't believe that a random person in the supermarket, a complete stranger, had called me 'darling'.

After about six weeks living in the Yellow House, we still had not heard anything from the UK-based agency that had organised our move to Australia. I emailed them and asked for an update. Two days later, I learned that our container had been accidentally unloaded in Hong Kong. They apologised for this mistake and advised that it would be another three weeks until we could expect our belongings. Luckily, we had booked the rental furniture for three months! At the end of October 2008, our belongings finally arrived at our doorstep. We could direct the bulk of it to our new home that we had bought in the meantime. Fortunately, it had two double garages, which ended up stacked with boxes and furniture to the roof. And I thought that everything happens for a reason.

At Christmas 2008, we finally moved in our house in Clontarf, which was only a short walk from the Yellow House, and I couldn't wait to furnish and decorate it. We had just finished a big renovation to transform the dated property into a more contemporary home. It took me almost three months to unpack and sort out all our belongings stored in the garage. Even though I had de-cluttered and discarded a lot of things in Wiesbaden, I still found items which made me wonder why we had shipped them around the world, such as snow boots, winter coats, and curtains from our previous home.

Eventually, the boxes disappeared and their contents found a place in our five-bedroom property. When we decided to put the red sofa in our study downstairs, I had no idea that it would become such a significant place for me eight years later.

LISTEN TO YOUR HEART

"The pathway to healing occurs when you love yourself so much that the darkness from the past can no longer co-exist with your faith in the light of the present moment."

Gabrielle Bernstein, The Universe Has Your Back

****

The first week after moving out of our bedroom was a rollercoaster of emotions.

On Tuesday, I poured my heart out to my coach about how miserable I felt since I had spoken to my husband. She again reminded me to be compassionate with myself and that we had discussed this would not be an easy conversation without consequences. She also encouraged me, out of fairness to him, to set clear boundaries at home and stand firm with them. We discussed that I would not accompany him to party invitations or other functions where I felt uncomfortable playing the role of the loving wife. At the same time, I decided only to reveal myself to the people who had earned my trust in the past. As always, I left my coaching session strengthened and with more confidence to move forward on my chosen path.

The same day, I saw a Council family lawyer to understand the legal aspects of a separation. If I decided to follow this path, I wanted to be able to make an informed decision. The lawyer was a friendly, middle-aged man, who explained the steps that needed to be taken in case of a separation. He also handed me a couple of brochures and a step-by-step workbook to use as a guideline for the extensive process of property settlement. I thanked him and left the consultation feeling much better prepared for what was looming on the horizon.

On Thursday night, it happened to be our last workshop session. We mainly shared our learnings and takeaways, and some women got quite emotional when they realised how much they had changed during the course of the workshop. There was a common theme of simplicity that emerged in the comments and stories we shared.

'Since I decided to stop disregarding my body and follow my inner wisdom, I make decisions from this place of love and stand firm in my decisions, even if they upset the people around me initially,' one woman said.

'I am enough as I am, I don't worry anymore that my hair is looking good if I'm going out somewhere,' was another revelation.

'I came to the realisation that I don't need anyone or anything to be happy. I am enough.'

I shared that the session with Jean Gamble on disregard and the presentation of Dr Michael Serafin about the physiological and emotional aspects of menstruation and menopause had made me reflect a lot on my life and how I had treated my body in the past 35 years. At some point, Michael had said: 'I am always surprised how many women come to me and have no idea what's going on in their body.'

During the workshop, I made the conscious decision to listen more often to my heart rather than my head and let go of the old habit of finding logical arguments for a decision that felt wrong. Although a creative soul, I am a very organised person who likes structure and to know where I am going. I am a hard worker and can get things done in a timely and efficient manner. This is how I was brought up and what I learned every single day from my parents. Making decisions from the head space has ruled most of my life. When I had finished school, I was drawn to study interior architecture and work in a creative field, however, I didn't have the courage to follow through with it and, therefore, came up with a list of arguments why it was better to study something else. I suppressed my true calling out of fear and a lack of belief in myself.

Twenty years later, in my 40s, I regretted my decision after I discovered how much I loved the Colour & Design Diploma course at the International School of Colour and Design in Sydney and how much it filled up my well. It is not that I hated my career in public relations but my heart and soul craved for more creative expression in my work and private life.

One thing I learned is to encourage my sons to listen to their heart when choosing their career path instead of looking for the jobs where they most likely will earn the most money. 'Follow your passion' was not something that was handed down to me. Both my parents were forced into jobs they hated and didn't have the courage to go for what they would have loved to do. I have learned that our true calling is going to haunt us throughout our life if we keep suppressing it. And that there will always be that nagging feeling that we are not living our best life, that there is something else out there for us. In the worst case, this can result in chronic illness because we keep ignoring the signals of our body.

MY CREATIVE JOURNEY

It was my mother who introduced me to the opera and art exhibitions when I was a teenager. I felt drawn to the world of the Creative Arts but lacked the courage to pursue a career in that field. Although my parents didn't force me to take over their business, they demonstrated to me every day that if I wanted a different life than theirs, it was best to find a high-income job rather than following a passion that might end up in unemployment and disappointment. So I buried my interest in interior architecture and studied, like a lot of my peers, business management, which led me into a career in public relations.

In 2005, when I was on maternity leave with my second son, Valentin, I made my first attempt at painting. We spent a couple of weeks in a holiday resort with an artist's studio. I loved playing with colours and textures on a canvas and kept painting at home, but never attended art classes.

My creative journey gained momentum in Australia in 2009 when Valentin turned four and could take the school bus with his brother, which saved me two hours of travel time every day. It was an enormous relief, and I finally could start thinking what I wanted to do with my life Down Under.

My plan was to study visual arts at our local TAFE (Technical and Further Education). I had researched and enrolled in a part-time course scheduled to start in February 2009. I couldn't wait to go back to school and immerse myself into a new venture.

A few weeks before the course was due to commence, the phone rang. 'We are sorry, but we have to cancel the part-time Visual Arts course due to an insufficient number of students,' a voice at the other end of the line explained. You can come to our full-time course if you like.'

The full-time course, however, was not an option, as I wanted to look after my sons in the afternoon. I had to find something else. After six months of driving the boys to school every day, doing the shopping and housework in between, my brain was hungry for a new challenge. I longed for something meaningful, something I was passionate about.

As I had to let go of the idea to study at TAFE, I decided to look at other options in the visual Aarts world and enrolled in a drawing class at Julian Ashton Art School where I studied drawing busts in the next three months. After finishing this course, I moved on to the National Art School and booked Painting En Plein Air for the second term. We met every Saturday in Sydney's Eastern suburbs to paint in the beautiful Nielsen Park.

My next project was a large-scale collage, which I finished during an art class in Manly. It is called Flinders Ranges, inspired by our holidays in the spring break the same year. The work found a place in our lounge room and was a constant reminder of my first taste of the Australian outback.

Isn't it funny that I had to travel around the world to go to an art school? Or was it meant to be that way? The drawing classes made me aware how much I enjoyed tapping into the right side of my brain. Time seemed to fly when I worked with pencil, charcoal, or brushes. One thing the art classes have taught me is to look at every-day objects with different eyes; more closely, observing colours, shapes, and textures; seeing the beauty in everything that surrounds us.

At the end of 2009, a recommendation from a fellow art student directed me to the International School of Colour and Design in North Sydney. The next eighteen months I dived into the realm of colour theory and psychology, drawing and illustration, rug and card design, 3D modelling and planning colour schemes for residential and commercial projects.

Apart from immersing myself into the world of art and design, I also started going to a dance studio in Manly for a Latin cardio class, which soon became one of my weekly highlights. The instructor was a professional ballroom dancer and introduced us to the basic steps of ChaCha, Rumba, Samba, Mambo, Merengue, Salsa, and Rock'n'roll within a 45-min workout. I went there for about a year until, much to my disappointment, our instructor left the studio to concentrate on his dance classes in the city. Through the studio, I had met a Salsa teacher, who invited me to come along to a weekly Salsa social with group classes beforehand. He didn't have to ask twice, and I immersed myself in the world of Street Latin dancing. The Salsa socials not only became my weekly fitness program but also a welcome break from my every-day life. Until, about a year later, the venue had to cancel the events due to complaints from the neighbours. And I stopped dancing for the second time.

*****

In 2010, I found myself most of the time alone at home, juggling the household, the kids' commitments and my assignments for the design school. My husband's job required him to work the majority of the year in the UK and he would only return home for short periods of time. The longer this situation lasted, the unhappier I became. The design school emanated positive energy and had become my haven and happy place. At the end of the year, I finished my CERT IV in Colour and Design and continued with a Colour Design Diploma course. At my graduation, in June 2011, my husband was overseas, so I had to celebrate it alone amongst my fellow students and their partners.

After the course, I decided to start an interior design business and become self-employed for the first time in my life. To build a substantial client basis turned out to be much harder than I had anticipated without any background in the industry or work experience in Australia. So, I applied for a part-time job as sales consultant with an Australian furniture designer. Within a couple of weeks, I started working in one of their Sydney retail outlets for the next 13 months.

At the same time, I decided that I would specialise in helping empty nesters downsize their homes and create a happy home in a smaller space. In January 2014, I self-published Downsize with Style. In the following months, I invested all my time and energy in connecting with real estate agents, apartment developers, and retirement villages to promote my book. I gave many downsizing talks and workshops, the majority of them for free. I tried so hard to make this business work that I arrived at a point of desperation and resentment. My inner voice told me to stop but I didn't want to hear it.

Then, in October 2014, I came across a little red book, called Memento, a collection of questions about my life. It was this book that propelled me on a path of exploration and self-discovery because I had to leave many questions unanswered. My curiosity to explore my family history was sparked and my intention for 2015 manifested: I was going to research and write my life's story.

As I had no idea how to start, I decided to enrol in a six-week life writing class at the Australian Writers' Centre, which turned out to be a wise decision. Once the course was finished, I would get up every morning at 5 am to write before the kids woke up and my morning routine started. In the following months, I produced piece after piece and watched my life's story emerge.

I had also booked a weekend workshop at the National Art School, called Drawing and Memory, as I was curious to explore if I could come up with some drawings to illustrate my story. Armed with my book about the history of my home town and some other inspirational images, I entered the main gate of the premises on a sunny Saturday morning. The massive sandstone buildings of the old Darlinghurst Gaol have been a school for artists since 1843 and for me there was always something mysterious about them.

The course started with a short introduction from the teacher about memory, a combined process of recollection and imagination, and how famous painters and artists created works based on their memories. She emphasised that memorising is a creative process and that memory is malleable. Through drawing, we can investigate and explore our memories. She also introduced formal considerations such as material, space, tone and colour, gesture and mark making, scale and clarity. To manipulate the work, she encouraged us to use transparent layers of imagery, gestural marks, empty spaces, erased marks, or fragmentation; in other words to explore and play with the material.

'Layer the drawing in the same way your story is layered. Develop it as a chain of images.'

We headed over to the building with the drawing studios and set up our easels with large drawing boards. I started working with the book I had brought. I particularly liked some aerial shots of our suburb and a painting from 1931 by the German artist Otto Dill. For my drawing, which took most of the first day, I worked with willow and compressed charcoal on Canson paper. The next day, I arrived with a series of inspirational images and started drawing small illustrations. When the lecturer saw me, she challenged me and said:

'You can use the workshop as you want, but think about further material exploration on a larger scale while you finish this drawing.'

I followed her advice and clipped a coloured Canson paper in A2 on my board. With the charcoal in my hand, I stared at the blank paper for almost an hour determined to "let my brush write what it would" as the Sung dynasty writer Ou-Yang Hsiu recommended in one of his essays. I became more and more impatient, and the more I forced myself into drawing, the worse I felt. I read through my notebook from the writing course trying to find a hook, an angle, an inspiration. At some point, I drew several circles on my paper. But what next? Frustration started to build up, and I finally addressed the teacher.

'I'm stuck; I don't know how to develop this drawing further.'

'Are these yours?' She looked at some feathers on my table.

'Yes.'

'Why don't you use this beautiful object to overlay your circles by rubbing the shape of your feather over them?'

She took my rubber and started making some marks on the paper. The effect was stunning. All of a sudden, I saw the possibility of this drawing, how to express my love for feathers. While rubbing over the charcoal, I turned the drawing upside to approach it from another angle. After I was content with my result, I decided to glue the feather onto the paper as another layer. After one hour of drawing and rubbing, I felt euphoric with the outcome.

Inspired by this exploration, I clipped another A2 sheet of beautiful white Arches paper on my board. I revisited some of my inspirational objects and photographs and got hooked by a large key from my family home in Germany. I started drawing the key on butcher paper playing around with its shapes and details. At home, I had framed that key glued to an image of an old master painting. I liked the juxtaposition of this somewhat faded and blurred image with the metal of the object. I decided to create a blurred background on my paper and draw the object on top of it. The charcoal seemed to glide over the smooth, high-quality paper, which felt almost like fabric. Just concentrating on the negative spaces, a landscape of fascinating shapes and marks, some bold and strong, other subtle and mysterious, emerged.

When I had finished and stepped back to look at it, I couldn't believe my eyes. I had taken the line for a walk, as the Swiss-German artist Paul Klee used to say, letting the charcoal draw what it would, exploring the marks it left behind, thick and thin, swirling around, up and down, opaque and translucent, leaving negative spaces, going to the edge but not over, seeking turning points to head in a different direction, creating new shapes, courageous, persistent, discovering new paths, settling down for a moment but then, moving on, curious, exploring, dreaming, dancing.

'Thank you for pushing me into the right direction,' I expressed my gratitude to our lecturer at the end of the day.

'My pleasure,' she replied, 'sometimes it is just a matter of persisting and not giving up.'

*****

When my 50th birthday was coming up in May 2015, I considered everything from doing nothing to disappearing to my favourite yoga retreat for a week. Eventually, I decided to spend this day with people I like and at a place that means something to me.

'Where are you going to celebrate your special birthday?' Heather, my hairdresser, wanted to know while working with a monstrous round brush and the blow dryer to style my hair for my special day.

'We're going to the Art Gallery. I've booked a guided tour through the new photography exhibition, then we'll have lunch in the gallery's function space. First, I wondered if people would like it, and was a bit worried that it might be too busy on a Saturday morning, but then I decided to give it a go and do something different.'

'That's awesome,' Heather exclaimed. 'Your guests will love it!'

When we arrived at the gallery on my special day, it was bustling with visitors. I hugged and kissed my guests as they arrived. As it turned out, some of them had never been in the Gallery before; others remembered school excursions a long time ago. We followed our guide for almost an hour through the exhibition. Afterwards, we made our way to the function space at the rear end of the gallery foyer – a bright, elevated area with views over the gallery foyer on one side and the suburb of Woolloomoolloo on the other. The weather was perfect; a beautiful, sunny day, which made the stunning views even more spectacular.

A couple of sculptures seemed to be placed randomly along the walls. The restaurant had set up a long table decorated beautifully with photo collages of me as table runners, flowers in red, pink, and white, three glass cloches displaying large 5s and 0s, domino stones, playing cards, and old books underneath. It had been a lot of fun planning the decoration, and I had put together an online board with inspirational images for the event organiser.

My guests were a colourful bunch of people, as colourful as the flowers on the table. Apart from the family, there were friends from the German School as well as architects and designers I had met through work. There were old friends from my husband's time in the Australian Navy in the 70s and 80s. Most people didn't know each other; some made new friends on the day.

I was so happy that I had chosen the art gallery for my birthday party. The food was fantastic, people were chatting and laughing over the table. Everyone had a great time. My guests repeatedly pointed out how lovely the afternoon had been and what a fabulous location I had chosen. I was in excellent spirits feeling blessed and privileged on my special day. The only person missing was Mum. It reminded me of my wedding in 2001 where we also had to celebrate without her.

****

2015 was the year of milestone birthdays. In June, my father turned 80. We flew to Germany, and I took the chance to find out as much as possible about our family history. I had to step out of my comfort zone, as our relationship had always been distant and reserved, but I was so glad I made the effort. For the first time he told me about his experiences as a young boy in Nazi Germany and his dream that never came true.

My father attended the local primary school in Haardt with his first year being in 1941 when the Second World War ravaged the country.

'There was not a lot of learning in those days,' he remembered. 'Often we did not even unpack our school bags, as there were continuous air alarms and we had to run home immediately; this could happen several times during school hours, that were in the morning only.'

The school had a big red cross mounted on the roof indicating to the enemy that this building should be spared bombing. All the big buildings used to be primary targets for the hostile bombers. Eventually, the school was evacuated, and the children were allocated to private homes to receive some education.

My father's class teacher's name was Herr Zimmermann, and he was a member of Hitler's SS or Schutzstaffel, a private squadron and major paramilitary organisation during the Third Reich. Every morning, the children had to stand up – their right arm stretched out for the Hitler Salute – singing the Deutschland-Lied, the national anthem of Germany since 1922.

In 1944, at the age of nine, my father was conscripted to join Die Pimpfe, part of the Nazi Party's youth organisation Hitlerjugend, founded in 1922. From 1933 until 1945, it was the sole official youth organisation in Germany and partially a paramilitary grouping. All children had to report to the local council in the school building. They got uniforms, a blue one for winter including sturdy shoes and a brown one for summer. 'We had to appear for military exercises every Sunday morning. Proudly showing off our new outfit, we used to march along the Kaiserweg,' my father remembered.

The Kaiserweg was and still is today a popular walking track through the forest above the village with great views over the Rhine Plain. As a child, I used to walk there with my school class for an excursion or with my parents on a Sunday afternoon. I most enjoyed it in autumn when there were mountains of dried yellow chestnut leaves piling up along the way; I would walk straight through them kicking the leaves like a ball, so they were swirled up in front of me. To hear that my father had to walk there as a child for military exercises made me sad, and, I was wondering how I would have coped with being forced into Hitler's youth organisation. As he explained in 2015, he and his friends just marched along together feeling happy that they had brand new clothes and shoes to wear – a pure luxury in those days.

Attending the Sunday exercises was compulsory, and when my father did not appear one morning, the Jungschaftführer, the leader of my father's youth group, threatened my grandmother with locking my father up if he missed the exercise another time. Luckily, as the war ended in 1945, my father only had to stand this military drill for one year and avoided being conscripted into Hitler's army. One of my father's cousins was not as lucky; at the age of 17 he had to join the air force and died one year later.

Unfortunately, my paternal grandfather, Helmut, never came back from Russia, where he died from starvation at the age of 36 after being imprisoned in Tiflis in 1945.

'Because he publicly refused to join Hitler's party, they conscripted him to the army – despite that fact that he was a baker,' my father explained. 'Hitler had given the order that each village should have a baker to provide its population with food.'

After Hitler's Machtergreifung, members of the Nazi Party – Parteibonzen as they were called from the locals – would always be around and intimidate the public. A large part of the population was afraid of saying something and kept their mouths shut. "Very many Germans did not want him until the end and even most of those who voted for him freely did not want what he finally brought," the German writer and historian Golo Mann stated in his book The History of the Germans since 1789. My father was only ten years old when he lost his father, and I never saw my grandfather except in family photographs.

My paternal grandfather, Helmut Gauweiler and both my grandmothers, Karolina Wasem, my father's mother, and Wilhelmine Marx, my mother's mother, were born in 1909; the same year my great grandfather, Peter Gauweiler, started building our family home in Neustadt-Haardt.

My great grandfather was born Protestant in Gommersheim – a Catholic stronghold at the southern part of the Weinstrasse – in 1873. With the protestant reformation and Martin Luther's publication of the 95 Theses in 1517 triggering a political, religious, cultural and intellectual upheaval in Catholic Europe, the protestant belief started to spread in Germany. Haardt had always been protestant. It was only after the Second World War that Catholics started arriving in our village, being refugees of the war. With his plans to open a bakery, my great grandfather, Peter Gauweiler, decided to leave his place of birth. Being protestant in a catholic village was not a very promising start for his business. Catholic customers would not buy their bread from a protestant baker. When he visited friends in Haardt one day – according to my father's cousin – he discovered an empty corner block on the main road. This seemed to be the perfect place for his business venture, as Haardt was a purely protestant community. Shortly after, he sold his family home in

Gommersheim and moved with his wife Marie to Haardt. They started to build our family home in 1909 and moved in a year later. It was a big, three-storey house majestically sitting on a corner block on the main road, called Hauptstraße, at that time.

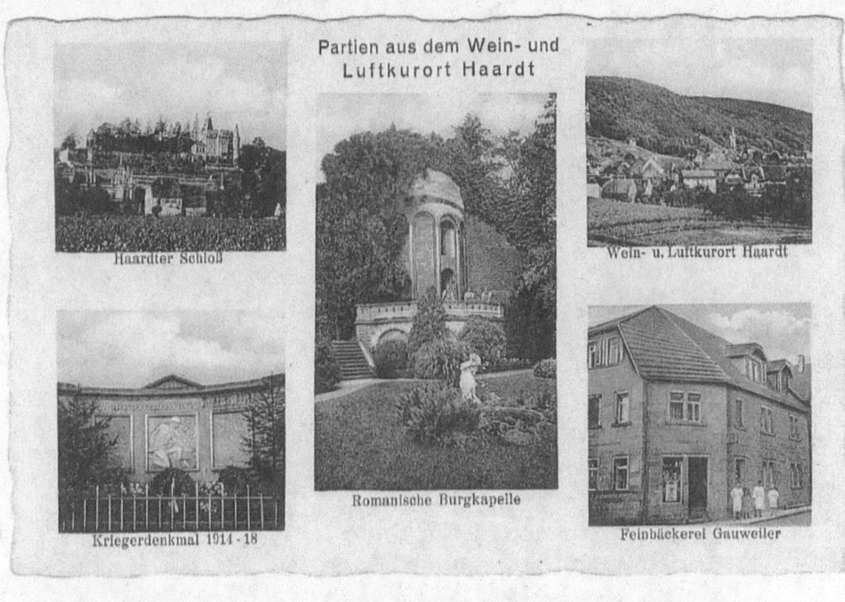

Our family home must have been something special by the time it was finished. I could not believe my eyes when I found a couple of faded postcards with our house being promoted amongst other tourist attractions. One of the cards – posted on the 6th of May 1911 – depicts our house as one of three images next to the greeting: Gruß von der Haardt, greetings from Haardt. The photographer focussed on the entrance of the shop and the small display window next to it. In front of the house, my great grandparents Peter Gauweiler and his wife Marie line up proudly with a group of people – men, women and children – who most probably belonged to the family or worked in the bakery. Above the house one can read the description: Bäckerei und Spezerei am schönen Eck von Peter Gauweiler – Peter Gauweiler's corner bakery and speciality shop.

The other postcard shows a collection of five smaller images, one of which was our family home, under the headline Partien aus den Wein- und Luftkurort Haardt – Impressions from the Wine and Climatic Spa Village Haardt.

*****

In the final months of World War II, the Western Allies invaded Germany. Some 1.6 million American troops had advanced deep into the country from the West, ultimately meeting the advancing Soviets at the Elbe River in the East.

'When the Americans arrived in Neustadt in 1945, they occupied our house and we had to leave. We slept in our neighbour's attic across the road for several months. Every afternoon at 5 pm, we had to close all the shutters and stay inside. When we finally were allowed to go back to our home, the entire house was messy and had been turned inside out,' my father told me. When they heard air raid warnings on the radio, my father often accompanied his maternal grandfather Ludwig Wasem – the local Luftschutzwart – around the village to check that all windows had been shaded, and no lights were left on. 'We witnessed how the Americans threw their phosphor bombs above the Rhine Plains; the sky was burning, painted in red and yellow.'

After the Americans, the French army took over. On the 5th of June 1945, the Allied Forces divided Germany in occupation zones and the French military set the rules and regulated people's lives in Neustadt. And my parents' families had to put up with the arbitrary power of the French army.

When they French soldiers arrived, they ransacked the homes of the locals. This is how I imagine it: a group of young French soldiers enter our cobblestoned backyard because the gate is open. They climb the four steps to the front door that is open as well, as it is summer, enter the house, look around, follow the narrow hall that leads to the kitchen on the right side. They enter the kitchen, ignoring my father – a ten-year-old boy watching the intruders with big eyes – and my grandmother, who is preparing a meal with what she could get for their food stamps. The young Frenchmen look around until they spot the little radio standing on top of the kitchen cupboard: a SABA radio, proof of German engineering quality. One points with his finger towards the radio, communicating to his comrade without words; they walk over to the cupboard, grab the radio, inspect it more closely, content with their find, and leave. A matter of minutes, and a precious item in our household was gone.

SABA, Schwarzwälder Apparate-Bau-Anstalt, was a manufacturer of high-end electronic equipment founded in Triberg in the Black Forest in 1923. Their radios were renowned for their technical features, a hand-built hardwood cabinet, brass trims, and a silk speaker cover.

'They came into the house, looked around, and just took everything they wanted,' my father summed up the scene seventy years later.

When I heard my father's stories in 2015, I realised how much his childhood experiences shaped his adult life. The fact that the family did not have enough to eat when he was growing up explained why later on my grandmother would always cook far too much food and encourage everyone to have another plate – even if we had all had enough. For many years, she used to cook for all of us, and we had leftovers almost every day. My father ended up being overweight and suffering from diabetes.

Like many other kids at that time, my father left school after eight years and started his apprenticeship at the age of fifteen in a bakery in the neighbouring suburb of Gimmeldingen. "As a baker, you will always have something to eat" was his mother's argument in support of following the footsteps of his father and grandfather. In those days, encouraging children to follow their true passion – in my father's case cars and motorbikes – was out of the question.

In our family home I looked through my parents' old photo albums and a cigar box full of photographs, which I had not opened for years. I found quite a few treasures: images of my parents as children, teenagers, and young adults. The most precious ones were faded portraits of my paternal grandfather and great grandfather with their families.

I also spoke with an 88-year old cousin of my father, who I had met at his birthday party. She not only knew the story of my great grandfather, born in 1873, who had to leave his place of birth to open his bakery and how he arrived in our village; with her help I was also able to reconstruct a small family tree from my father's side. She showed me a folder full of faded family photographs and newspaper cutouts, one of which was the obituary notice of my grandfather Helmut. She also told me that a man with the name of Friedrich Gauweiler had contacted her the year before, as he was researching his family history. There was a picture of him together with her and her husband. However, I didn't attach any importance to her story at the time.

I also interviewed Mum's brothers Klaus, Robert, and Helmut. We gathered in Helmut's apartment for afternoon coffee and cake. I had warned my uncles beforehand and had sent them a long list of questions to which I was seeking answers. My uncles told me their stories and what they remembered about their childhood together with my mother; how they survived the Second World War as young children; how Uncle Klaus had branded my mother one day. I even found out about a family secret that was hushed up for many years. We were chatting away, laughing and enjoying this sense of belonging, being woven together with an invisible thread, unbreakable. Faded photographs changed hands, and they had all brought images for me to take home to Australia. My fingers danced over my keyboard as I tried to capture their words while they spoke.

Another invitation led me to the house of a very good friend of my mother, whom I had not seen for over fifteen years. Linked through the same surname, but not related to us, they shared some stories about the rivalry between Protestants and Catholics in the history of the Palatinate region, triggered by the Protestant Reformation in 1517. The story that my father's cousin had told me about my great grandfather all of a sudden made much more sense. Researching my family history, I hoped to reconnect and engage my 13 and 10-year-old sons with their country of birth. After initial protests, and repeatedly emphasising how boring it was to visit yet another relative or acquaintance who might be able to shed some light on my past, Max admitted: 'You've learned a lot about your family over the weekend.' He even looked through the old family photographs and wanted to know who the people were.

Returning in 2015 to my family home, I realised that if this house had been any kind of home, it wasn't one any longer. Over the years, our house had become more and more abandoned. I moved out in 1985 when I started studying in Worms. Mum passed away in 1998. A few years later, my father stopped working, and the shop closed. My paternal grandmother died in 2000, Alfons in 2003. My father was the last resident in our house, which was waiting for its uncertain future, as he had sold it years ago - behind my back - with the right to live in it until his death.

Back home in Sydney, I added the new pieces to my life puzzle. A few weeks after our return, I found a large letter from Germany in my letterbox, posted from a small village near Neustadt by Friedrich Gauweiler. I was overwhelmed by its contents: an A4 folder with ten images of my grandparents and great grandparents, including the obituary notice of my grandfather Helmut cut out from the local newspaper in 1945. With teary eyes, I read his cover letter, in which he explained that Gretel, my father's cousin, had told him about my visit and asked him to send me some images and information about our family history. He also mentioned that he and his wife had been to Australia several times visiting family and friends in Melbourne, Brisbane, and Sydney. It took another four months, and more correspondence, to find out that Friedrich's great grandfather Christoph (1841 - 1926) and my father's great grandfather Georg-Heinrich (1843 - 1919) were brothers.

MIDLIFE MAYHEM

"People try to get away from it all – to the beach, to the mountains. You always wish that you could too. Which is idiotic: you can get away from it anytime you like. By going within."

Marcus Aurelius, Meditations

****

2016 had been one of those years. The word C H A N G E was prominently placed on my vision board and I was up for a rollercoaster ride.

Two years after self-publishing my book and trying to get my interior design business off the ground, I was exhausted to say the least. I had arrived at a point where I was sick of everything and everyone, just wanting to escape. I'd been so passionate about building my business that I'd worked more hours than I ever before. I convinced myself that I had to keep offering my services for free or at a ridiculously low price to gain more experience and put together a portfolio, to a point where it became hard to charge for the value I delivered. I felt frustrated and resentful. To keep up positivity and motivation on a daily basis became a Sisyphean task. To continue down the road I had been travelling would neither be sustainable nor fun.

As often before, I looked for some solace in my extensive book collection. My eyes rested on the blue-purple spine of The *Obstacle is the Way by Ryan Holiday*. Inspired by Marcus Aurelius and the concepts of Stoicism, the author provides a recipe book for dealing with all the obstacles that life throws in our way: mental, physical, emotional, and perceived obstacles. I started to think about how I could turn the obstacles to my advantage.

The year before, I had started to write house features and my stories were published in several design and lifestyle magazines.

Writing had always been part of my professional career, and I enjoyed it very much. Something inside me told me to pursue this path further. In March 2016, I let go of interior design apart from writing about it and relaunched my website focusing on content and copywriting. I brushed up my skills with a course at the Australian Writers Centre and became a member of a Facebook community for copywriters.

A month later, I received a letter from our council with an invitation to attend my citizenship ceremony on the 13 April 2016. After one year of filling out forms and waiting for approval, I would finally become Australian. As my husband was on a business trip and my sons declared that there was nothing more boring than coming along to my citizenship ceremony, I asked a friend to accompany me not to be alone on this milestone event in my life. Now, that the Australian passport was within reach, I started to feel a bit anxious. I wondered how I would feel becoming a citizen of another country. Would I lose my German identity? Would I feel insecure about where I belong? What would I say if someone asked me for my nationality? Would I feel more Australian than German if I stayed here for the rest of my life? In hindsight, none of my fears manifested and I feel privileged to be a citizen of both countries.

Mid-year, I stumbled into the unravelling phase of midlife without any warning. Several heavy bleedings I had never experienced in 35 years scared me to death. I consulted my GP. She looked at me with a cheeky grin on her face:

'How old are you?' - '51.'

'Hello, menopause,' she replied. When I didn't say anything, she continued:

'You're not the only woman who is oblivious of the symptoms that announce menopause. Most women have no idea what's going on until they are right in the middle of it.'

By mid-November, after an intense, emotional year, I suggested to my husband to spend the last week of the year at a boutique wellness retreat in the Byron Hinterland I had first discovered in 2009. I hadn't been there for over three years and remembered the promise I had given to the General Manager back in 2013 that it wouldn't take another four years until I returned. We booked the last available room for five nights.

When I browsed the spa menu to plan my treatments, I was intrigued by the Esoteric Breast Massage (EBM), as the menu explained that this treatment could alleviate menopausal symptoms. I booked it for the afternoon on our arrival day. It was the 27th of December 2016.

After the massage therapist had welcomed me in her treatment room, she said:

'This is a familiar face. You've been here before, haven't you?'

'Yes, twice. Last time in 2013, I had a treatment with you.'

Nicolette, the therapist, who I remembered as a lovely woman, explained to me the modality of the EBM and how healing it can be. It is only practised by women for women. I liked the idea of nurturing myself and reconnecting with my body and relaxed instantly to the magic of her hands. It was a very tender and gentle massage, and I found myself in a peaceful place of love and compassion.

After the treatment, we had a conversation about the essence of a woman and how important it is to honour our sacred self every single day. I told her that I loved going to my yoga classes, as I cherished the peace and stillness that this space held for me.

'You don't have to go anywhere to find this stillness,' Nicolette assured me, 'it is right within you. You only have to reconnect with your body. It is ok to be vulnerable and fragile – that doesn't mean you are weak – and you can still do all the things you need to do in your daily life, one thing at a time.' I captured her words in my journal that afternoon.

I was not aware at the time that she had carefully opened the door to a place deep within me which I had disconnected from a long time ago and which I would discover in all its beauty on the last day of the year.

A NEW BEGINNING

"Have the courage to follow your heart and intuition. They somehow already know what you truly want to become. Everything else is secondary."

Steve Jobs

****

In the first weeks of 2017, I found it hard to slip back into my every-day life. Only days after our return, I sat in my study overlooking leafy gardens with Middle Harbour shimmering through the trees. My red sofa had become my favourite writing place. The brownish red with an undertone of black blended beautifully with the colours in the artwork on the wall behind it. It was one of my paintings of a blooming tree inspired by a Japanese art exhibition at the Art Gallery of New South Wales. I usually had a notebook, my printed manuscript, and a cup of tea on a small tray beside me. This was my writing zone, normally a space of contentment.

The refreshing morning air was streaming in through the large door that opened to a timber deck outside. I gazed at the horizon where I could see the first beams of sunlight reflecting from the houses on the other side of the harbour. I heard the distant noise of cars crossing the Spit Bridge travelling into the city, the chatter, laughing and singing of the myna birds, kookaburras and magpies.

At 5:30 am, my husband and our teenage sons were still asleep. I cherished the early morning hours when the house was quiet and peaceful. It was the perfect time to write.

Everything on the surface appeared unchanged. But nothing was as it used to be.

Fragments of memories emerged as I listened to the early morning sounds. I found myself in a vortex of insecurities, which tormented my life on a daily basis. My mind replayed the same 90 minutes over and over again. 90 minutes that had turned my life upside down and opened a mysterious door to a new world – unknown and frightening but full of potential.

My writing space had always radiated a sense of comfort, security and belonging. It was a safe haven, a shelter. Now, I wasn't so sure anymore; my heart told a different story.

I didn't know with whom to talk. Who would understand what I was going through? I visualised my best friends and imagined how they would react when I told them what had happened. I was in a total mess, not able to concentrate on much. Over and over again, my mind replayed my experiences at the retreat culminating in the Kahuna massage.

Was it all coincidences? The more I reflected on the sequence of events at the retreat, the more I came to the conclusion that it was meant to happen. My mind kept turning in circles desperately trying to find answers. At the end of an excruciating week I went through all my business contacts to find someone to talk to. When I came across a family coach, I remembered my brief conversation with this woman at a networking event a couple of months before and that I had instantly felt at ease with her. I also knew that I wanted a neutral person, someone who didn't know me. I sent her an email with my enquiry.

In hindsight, it was a wise decision, as I did a lot of very challenging emotional work with her and don't know whether I would have revealed my experiences, thoughts, and emotions with the same authenticity and rawness to a person who was close to me. And because of my vulnerability and our professional relationship, I got so much out of my coaching sessions. I always felt safe in her presence. I know that without her I would not have coped with the challenges that I had to face in the months ahead.

When Karina got my email, she replied on the same day that she would love to meet me and listen to my story. I was relieved beyond measures that I could finally share my experiences with someone. When we met I spoke for almost an hour about what had occupied my mind for days on end.

When I was finished, Karina grinned at me:

'You know what? You are in a hell of an exciting time! This guy has freed your Goddess, who must have been hidden for many years. He invited her to come out and dance with him. He uncovered your sensual, sexual, emotional self. And because she was locked away for such a long time, you had such a profound experience. You have just discovered your innermost self, your sacred wisdom, your full potential as a loving woman.'

I digested her words and suddenly everything seemed to make much more sense. I remembered my very first Esoteric Healing treatment with Nicolette in 2013 after which she had told me that she could sense many suppressed emotions in my body. At that time, I was not ready to hear it and ignored her advice. This time, she had given me a business card of an esoteric healer in Sydney, 'in case you want another session.'

Nicolette's words kept ringing in my ears: 'To be vulnerable doesn't mean that you are weak. You don't have to be strong all the time.'

A few days after my initial conversation with Karina, I found myself in the treatment room of Nicolette's friend in Sydney and we chatted about my experiences at the retreat. She also emphasised the importance of nurturing ourselves, which has a lot to do with our relationship with our body and how we feel about it.

After my session, she invited me to a six-week workshop called Understanding Menstruation & Menopause organised by the College of Universal Medicine in March 2017. I booked my place the next day.

<u>Coaching Sessions (I)</u>

Mid-January 2017, I attended my first coaching session. Karina had sent me several pages of questionnaires to fill out and reflect on myself, my love life, my family life and what I wanted to get out of the sessions with her. When I filled the pages with words, I became aware that this profound spiritual experience had been like an earthquake deep down at the bottom of the ocean causing a wave that would slowly start to build and become faster and higher the closer it approached the shore to eventually hit the landscape with devastating power and leave destruction behind. Nothing could stop it.

We spoke for almost two hours and I again expressed my feelings to her. Towards the end of our session, built-up emotions broke through and I couldn't hold back my tears. She emphasised that it would be my role as the teacher in the family to start implementing changes in my communication and behaviour, so that my sons would learn how to talk to the future women in their lives in a loving and respectful way. She also encouraged me to stop being reasonable all the time, accommodating everything for everyone in the family and putting myself last.

At the end of our session, Karina handed me a word card deck and asked me to pull a card, I shuffled the small pack of rectangle cards and chose:

SIMPLICITY

'What does this mean to you?' Karina wanted to know. I looked at the word and couldn't stop the tears again. The first thing that came into my mind were my yoga classes and how often the teachers encouraged us to keep things simple, to concentrate on each single breath, a simple act of reconnecting with ourselves.

At the end of our first session, she handed me her Welcome Pack with a gift: A Butterfly Oracle Card Set for Life Changes by Doreen Virtue. Each card depicted a delicate, colourful butterfly,

"The perfect symbol of beauty when you undergo life changes," as the guidebook explained.

In the evening, I had a closer look at the cards. The guide book explained that you can't go wrong with your card choices, as the universal Law of Attraction supports you in receiving the right card with an answer to your question.

My curiosity was sparked, and I read the instructions for three-card messages. I prayed that I would be able to follow my mantra for 2017 practising love and compassion, first and foremost with myself but also with those around me. I shuffled the deck and pulled three cards. I placed the first card to my left; it revealed something about the event that had triggered my question. The second card pointed to the here and now and what I needed to work on. The third card, on the right side, stood for the immediate future if I continued to follow my chosen path.

The first card:

SUPPORT

You received this card because you've been accustomed to doing everything yourself, and now it's time to request and receive help. This is a valuable life lesson that will allow you to grow in every area, so think of it as an investment.

The middle card:

YOU ARE STRONGER THAN YOU KNOW

Challenging situations show you your inner strength, especially when you seem to have no choice but to handle the matter directly. This card is encouraging you to keep going and to call upon the deep well of strength that God has given you.

The card of my immediate future:

BE TRUE TO YOU

You drew this card because of an inner conflict. You are struggling to make a decision about your next actions. You worry whether following your desired path is the right choice, and how doing so will impact others.

What did all the cards tell me? Would I find rekindled love? With myself? With my husband? With someone else? Would I reconnect with Christianity? Where would my growing interest of the Buddhist way of life lead me? Where would I live in the future? What would I do?

I felt overwhelmed as if suffocating under a dark, heavy cloak. When I finally fell asleep that night, I dreamt that I was telling my closest friends about my decision to start a new chapter of my life.

The next day, thoughts kept shooting through my mind. Flashes of possibilities. It was almost unreal how the Universe kept speaking to me. My body told me that the time had come to reconnect with my Christian faith.

HOW TO WALK INTO CHURCH

"Three relationships:

1. With the body you inhabit;
2. With the divine, the cause of everything in all things;
3. With the people around you."

Marcus Aurelius, Meditations

***

On Sunday, the 22 January 2017, I attended my first traditional service at Seaforth Anglican church. I had spoken about going to Sunday church since our arrival in Australia in 2008 but never did. Life had taken over and apart from attending the service on Christmas Eve, I never made it a priority.

However, after the Christmas evening service in 2016, the church had distributed a small present to each family: a pocket-sized book called How To Walk Into Church. I was intrigued by the title and read it in one sitting the next day. The book offered recommendations on how to prepare to walk into church, what to do before and after the service and how to make the most out of a Sunday church visit.

The one thing that struck me most was the recommendation "we should walk into church praying about where to sit." According to the author, this attitude "expresses perfectly what sort of thing church is, and what we are doing there."

Whenever we pray, we have faith; faith in God, the universe or in whatever else we believe. Secondly, the author elaborated further that by praying where to sit, "we are putting ourselves into the right frame of mind towards each other."

With this in mind, I entered the church building that Sunday. I had faith that the universe would guide and protect me and show me the right way. I was also wondering what would happen when I joined the community going by myself for the first time. According to the little book, I should be met with open arms and people should approach and welcome me.

I climbed up the flight of stairs that lead to the entrance area of the very simple yellow brick building. At the door, I was greeted by a member of the congregation who asked me if I had a name tag. When I said no, he asked me how I would like to be called.

"Bettina is my name," I replied, and he wrote a new name tag for me.

I went inside and chose a seat on the fourth pew from the front, which was still empty. Although a normal Sunday, there was quite a crowd present: many pews were populated with families with toddlers and primary school children; there were couples in all age groups and balanced mix of men and women. What struck me were the number of teenagers and young adults attending the service. In our local church in Germany, on a normal Sunday, you would mainly meet elderly people.

My eyes wandered through the interior, which was in a similar simple and de-cluttered style as the exterior. The blue carpet on the floor together with the emerald green upholstery fabric on the pews radiated a sense of calmness. The only decoration were eight rectangular coloured glass windows depicting scenes from the Bible. There were little descriptions next to each window, and I had a closer look at the one next to me. It revealed Archangel Michael as the protagonist in the picture.

I sat down and caught the eye of the minister, who I knew from the Christmas services. When he saw my unfamiliar face, he came straight over to me and introduced himself:

'Hi, I'm Jamie. I'm the minister here. Welcome!'

'Hi, I'm Bettina.'

'Is this your first time at our church?' he asked.

'No, we usually come at Christmas every year, but this year I made it a New Year resolution to attend the regular Sunday service more often.'

'Great! We have a traditional service at 8:15 in the morning and a more contemporary service at 4:45 in the afternoon,' he explained.

Not long after the minister went back to the lectern to prepare the service, a lady sitting in the pew to the right to me stood up, smiled and introduced herself.

'Welcome! My name is Fiona. Are you visiting today?'

I explained that I lived in the nearby suburb of Clontarf, for over eight years and that I had decided to attend the Sunday service more regularly. She was very pleased to hear this and invited me to join the congregation for morning tea in the community centre next door. She also encouraged me to fill out one of the 'Connection Cards' that were scattered along the pews.

More people approached me as the service went along. Everyone was welcoming me with open arms into their community. I met a couple of neighbours from our suburb and had the pleasure to chat with the minister's wife during morning tea. An hour after the service had finished, I was still chatting to the church community. I felt warmly welcomed by a group of strangers and decided to come back more often.

<u>Coaching Sessions (II)</u>

I couldn't wait to see Karina again; to tell her about everything that had happened in the past seven days. Things seemed to fall into place guided by an invisible force.

'I seem to drift towards spiritual people. This is where I feel at home, at ease; these are people I want to hang out with,' I explained. I knew that my yoga practice over the previous six years had played a significant part in this development. I felt more connected with myself, I looked at things differently, my priorities had changed. And, as a consequence, my emotions had changed.

'At the same time, I feel that I drift further and further away from my husband like a buoy that is carried away by the waves, slowly but constantly,' I confessed.

Karina congratulated me for taking responsibility for my life and encouraged me to be true to myself whatever decisions I would make and share what I wanted with no expectations of any reactions. I knew that in the past years I had often suppressed my emotions to avoid conflict and that it would require all my courage to be true to myself more often. I also felt deep inside me that it would only be a question of time until the inevitable conversation with my husband would have to happen. I didn't feel at home in our marriage anymore.

INKLINGS

"With courage, there is the willingness to take chances and to let go of former securities."

David R. Hawkins, Letting Go

*****

During the month of February, the minister focused on the theme Ignite Your Passion for his weekly sermons. The first Sunday, he spoke about what passion is, what it means for different people and how we can express our passion for God. On the following Sunday, he contemplated on how we can give God our best in our everyday life.

On the third Sunday, he spoke about vulnerability. At the end of 2016, my vulnerability had opened the gate to a pathway towards higher consciousness. By now I knew that it was my courage to step out of my comfort zone and surrender completely to the hands of my skilled massage therapist that had made my spiritual awakening possible. Vulnerability combined with trust had shown me a new source of happiness deep within me, an experience of inner peace. For the first time, I had encountered true spiritual awareness, a profound occurrence that had triggered the desire to change my life.

"On the level of courage, we are willing to take responsibility for our religious and spiritual position," David R. Hawkins writes in Letting Go. The author explains the different levels of consciousness by using the Scale of Emotions he developed. Each level of consciousness is located on a scale of energetic power ranging from 1 - 1000. The highest level (1000) means Enlightenment. As examples, he names Jesus Christ and Buddha, who reached this energetic level. The feeling of shame, on the other hand, is located on the very bottom of the scale (20) and represents bare survival. The author further emphasises that the level of courage at an energetic power (200) is the turning point between negative and positive energy and that "the level of courage is the energy of integrity, being truthful, empowerment, and having the capacity to cope."

I devoured this book, which Karina had recommended to me, as I found myself again and again on its pages. "We can utilise courage to reinforce our desire to grow beyond our present state, because on this level, we are already getting inklings that there is something within us that we had hitherto unsuspected. These inklings are indicated by those sudden episodes of perfect stillness and peace in which we have great clarity, understanding, and heightened sensitivity to beauty."

I was instantly transported back to the relaxation area of the spa where I had spent an hour after my Kahuna massage to cherish this new sense of consciousness that permeated my body. I remembered seeing the beauty in everything around me: the flowers, the stones, the birds, the afternoon sun shimmering in the delicate fabric of the orange sheers that decorated the place.

Only now after I read David Hawkins' book did I begin to understand what had happened during my massage. At the time, I couldn't articulate it. I sensed that it had something to do with Jay's skills as Kahuna bodyworker. I felt that it was also the music that underpinned this experience. Only through reflecting on my experiences in the weeks after, through investigating further did I find out that my therapist, his kindness and compassion, the music were only the circumstances that allowed this deep connection to happen. They paved the way for my mind to become still. As a consequence, they allowed me to dip into a space beyond the incessant chatter of my mind, the endless repetition of thoughts, memories, worries, emotions, and sensations. In this moment, time seemed to stand still, and I felt this deep connection, this oneness, with Jay. I had tasted something so sweet and precious that I would never forget it.

I realised that my wish to join my local church community and to reconnect with a higher power was a direct result of my increased awareness for myself. I was curious to discover more about me through weekly religious and spiritual practices. I wanted to find out how to return to this realm of peace and inner freedom. I knew deep in my heart that I had made the first steps and that it would only be a matter of time and persistent practice until I climbed the 'Scale of Emotions'.

<u>Coaching Sessions (III)</u>

Time seemed to fly when I had my sessions with Karina. I cherished our conversations as they were meaningful and encouraging. They also gave me the confidence to move forward on this new path that I had chosen.

The most important takeaway from my third session was to set strong boundaries to protect myself from my husband's and my sons' disrespectful conversations. The clash a couple of weeks before where I had left the dinner table and disappeared for three hours was only the start. I had felt hurt, disrespected, and angry and the only way to remove myself from the conversation was to leave.

After discussing the incident with Karina, I decided to talk to the boys to tell them why I reacted the way I did and to assure them that I didn't want to frighten them or threaten them in any way. I wanted them to know that it was important to talk in a kind and respectful way to me and all the future women in their life.

I was the one who needed to take action to improve the communication in our family. Only with trust and vulnerability paired with courage and faith would I be able to initiate change.

At the end of our session, I drew a card from the Archangel deck. When I shuffled the cards, one fell on the floor – Archangel Michael. It was the third time that I came across him after my first Angel Card reading in February 2016 and the discovery of his picture in one of the coloured glass windows in the church.

The card revealed the following:

Through this card, Archangel Michael is making his presence known to you. He is the symbol of true courage, stemming from knowing that God's love is the only power there is. Michael is letting you know that, as you make changes in your life and as you encounter challenges, you are safe and secure. God and the angels help you stay true to yourself during trying times.

Together with Karina, I summarised the main takeaways from this third session in a long list of 'homework' for the next couple of weeks. The most important point was setting strong boundaries. The second task on my list was to speak to the boys about the Friday night incident. The third point was to be aware of how I acted and reacted on the scale of being reasonable and unreasonable.

When I looked up the meaning of Archangel Michael at home, I learned that he "is the epitome of strength and valour and intervenes miraculously to save lives and protect our bodies, loved ones, vehicles, belongings, and reputation." Regarding spirituality, he protects us from fear and fear-based energies.

I realised that it was my fear of being vulnerable, of not knowing how others would react, of hurting someone that had held me back to address many issues in the past.

I then discovered that Archangel Michael helps people to know the purpose of their lives and guides them towards the next steps triggering important life changes. His colours are royal purple, royal blue and gold. Colours I like very much.

<u>Conversations (I)</u>

The opportunity to talk to Max opened up the next day when he stayed home from school, sick. I prepared myself repeating the words in my head several times before I went up to his room with an uncomfortable feeling in my stomach:

'Max, do you have five minutes for me? I'd like to talk to you.'

'Yes,' he looked at me curiously.

'You remember the Friday night at dinner one and a half weeks ago, when I left the table because Dad disagreed with what I said?'

'Mmh, yes,' he replied after a few seconds.

'I just wanted to let you know that I felt very hurt and angry because your Dad spoke again to me in a very disrespectful way. It happened before, and I always swallowed my emotions. I have decided that from now on I won't tolerate that any longer. If he, you, or your brother do not speak kindly to me, I will finish the conversation and leave.'

Max didn't look at me while I was talking; he played with a little Lego figure in his hands, but I could sense that he listened attentively.

'I didn't want to scare or frighten you,' I continued 'and I also spoke with Dad the next morning. But I want you to know that women do not want to be talked to in a disrespectful way. No matter if you speak with a girl in your school, your future girlfriend or wife or any other woman in your professional life – they all want to be treated kindly and with compassion. It is important to me that you know this, as I want you to be happy in your life.'

Then, I paused, and all my 15-year-old son said was 'ok'.

We gave each other a big hug before I left his room. A couple of weeks later, I explained myself to my younger son, who showed a similar reaction. The only question he asked was where I had been.

Coaching Sessions (IV)

I started my fourth session with Karina by reporting what I had ticked off my homework list from the previous meeting: I had spoken to my boys about the Friday night; I had spoken with Martin regarding the roster for the kids to help with the household chores. I had prioritised the dinner with the church ladies over the parent night at my son's school, which my husband attended. I kept avoiding awkward situations with Martin, such as going out for dinner, for the time being.

We then spoke about the five languages of love - *Acts of Service*, *Words of Affirmation*, *Receiving Gifts*, *Quality Time* and *Physical Touch*, and how everybody speaks a different love language and reacts to a different one. I knew instantly, which of the love languages applied to our family. My younger son and I expressed our love through touch, whereas my older son and my husband seemed to appreciate acts of service and words of affirmation. If I looked at our family life with the love languages in mind, I could see why we often dealt with misunderstandings or miscommunication. The central question for me was: What did I need in order to feel loved?

There was, however, another topic that I had carried around with me for many years without resolving it: my money beliefs. I had started to work on this with a business coach a couple of years before. I knew about my *Sacred Money Archetypes* and which positive affirmations to use to introduce change. However, I didn't feel that I had made a big progress.

'These affirmations didn't come from you, therefore you didn't fully own them,' Karina explained.

What did I need to let go in order to make real change happen? As our conversation went along, the topic of 'Identifying Beliefs' and letting go of negative emotions crystallised as becoming the next step in my work with her.

'This is where real change happens,' Karina explained. 'In this very deep work, we will look at what happened in your childhood, at your mum and dad, the people who influenced you while you grew up. We will identify events and incidents that made you adopt certain beliefs. We will look at the origin of mannerisms that come up for you over and over again in your adult life. Then, we will acknowledge them and let them go, so that you can move forward with your new life and make a confident decision from your heart about your future.'

I knew this was the path I needed to follow even if it would be uncomfortable.

RESPECT TRUMPS HARMONY

"Change your thoughts, change your life."

Lao-Tzu

*****

It was the middle of March and I was still dazzled by what had unfolded in the first ten weeks of the year. Apparently unrelated events, learnings from my coaching sessions and my card readings seemed to plug into each other like puzzle pieces. Some days I felt quite overwhelmed and had to let go of the feeling of having to control and understand everything. An invisible force seemed to pull me forward inviting me to go with the flow.

<u>Coaching Sessions (V)</u>

At our fifth session, Karina greeted me with the question how the past week had been and how I was going in general.

"You know, I see it very clearly now. My marriage is over," The words just tumbled out of my mouth.

"I was waiting for you to tell me that," she replied calmly.

I started telling her about the recent delivery of our family portraits. At the retreat, I had received a gift voucher for a family photo shoot as a thank you for being a returning guest. Initially intrigued by the idea of having some new family photos done after more than ten years, I had booked the photo shoot at the end of January without thinking about what this would entail. When the photographer asked me to stand next to my husband and put my arm around him, I had to fight the resistance in my body. However, as I didn't want to risk a scene in the studio, I kept playing my role as the happy wife.

When the five photographs arrived at our home, we had a quick look at them; but none of us seemed to be very enthusiastic about displaying them. I knew that I was not the happy wife that smiled at me from the picture. How long would I keep living the lie? Would I be courageous enough to speak up eventually? Would I be willing to take the risk and start a new chapter of my life, a second time after 2008?

The thought of facing a divorce paralysed me. I didn't know anything about family law, let alone how to find a lawyer that I could trust. I felt overwhelmed not knowing where to start. Karina suggested to do some research into the legal aspects of separating and also talk to some of my girlfriends, who went through a divorce in the past. As usual, I followed her advice concentrating on one step after the other and not worrying about the future.

The other thing we agreed upon was to look closer into my beliefs and habits triggered through my upbringing and family history. Karina prepared me that this would be much deeper work and our sessions would be shorter, as I would have to do more homework and spend time to work through the discussions afterwards. Although I was a bit apprehensive how I would cope with these modalities, I knew it was the only way moving forward.

<u>Conversations (II)</u>

On the 14th March 2017, Max's 15th birthday, my husband and I had an appointment with Max's form teacher. Our son had just started Year 9 and we wanted to meet his new teacher, who would be the his main contact person for the next couple of years.

Unfortunately, Max's performance at school had deteriorated in the past year, and he didn't show any enthusiasm to do more than just the bare minimum. One of the issues that the teacher brought up was the way he kept his school diary. In his usual, efficient way of approaching tasks, he would only jot down bullet points for his homework and tick them off once done. The teacher, however, required the boys to keep a daily record of what they had learned in each lesson. As he explained, this was to deepen their learning experience. Additionally, it would be a chance for us to start a conversation with him about his work at school.

While he kept talking, I suddenly felt that I had let down my son in the past 12 months. I had watched him retreat more and more into his secluded world of adolescence, dominated by computer games and artificial realities, where there seemed to be no space for me. We had stopped talking. And the little talking that was happening was superficial, small talk, meaningless words.

All my attempts to talk to him about anything mostly ended in heated arguments and unpleasant conversations with both of us screaming at each other. As a consequence, I had swapped the driver's seat with a comfortable back seat and merely watched. This comfort, of course, came with the price of a deeper separation between my son and me.

Hadn't I just devoured all those books about kindness, compassion, and vulnerability? About daring greatly to make a difference in our lives and the lives of the people we love? At that moment, in the school's meeting room, I knew that I had to jump back into the driver's seat, be a leader and help my son through this challenging time of adolescence. If I wanted to teach him anything about kindness, compassion, and vulnerability, I would have to seek those difficult conversations and keep doing them repeatedly.

Through my work with Karina, I had become aware of the absence of meaningful conversations in our household. And I had already experienced the beautiful feeling of relief and contentment after a short but meaningful conversation with my son a few weeks earlier.

'Have you ever involved Max in any decisions that had a direct impact on him?' the teacher asked.

I made a mental note about compiling a list of conversations I would need to have with my son in the coming weeks. It became apparent that, in the past years, we had made decisions above his head without asking him what he thought, felt, or wished. As we couldn't turn back the time, I was even more determined to change my behaviour in the future.

'Respect always trumps harmony,' I remembered a presentation at a networking event the week before. In the afternoon, I wrote a list of conversations to have with my son with the first one on that same day when Max returned from school.

He had texted me in the morning, quite upset about his birthday invitation that we didn't expect any presents and rather appreciated a contribution from the parents towards the accommodation costs for the overnight stay in Canberra. My husband had organised a trip to the capital with him and seven boys on the coming weekend. As it turned out, he had changed the initial draft without asking Max.

'How did you feel when you read Dad's invitation?' I opened the conversation.

'I was a bit disappointed, as I would have liked to get some presents.'

'I understand, I am sorry, that we didn't ask your opinion about this idea.'

'When we went with Lachie to Canberra last year, we all gave him presents,' he continued.

'Yes, I know. It was very disrespectful not to involve you in this decision. We'll make sure that we talk to you in the future when decisions directly impact on you.' - 'Ok.'

COACHING SESSIONS (VI-VIII)

"It'll be ok, Mum."

Max

*****

With curiosity and anticipation, I arrived at Karina's home for our next coaching session. As usual, Karina asked me if I wanted to share what had happened in the past three weeks since we had last seen each other.

The day before, I had attended the yearly parent-teacher interviews in Max's school. I was positively surprised about the feedback we received. His teachers unanimously said that they enjoyed having him in class, that he was disciplined and diligent, that he delivered his assignments on time, contributed to class with comments and questions. However, they also pointed out that he was easily distracted and often just stopped working because something else had caught his attention. They encouraged him to stay focused in order to work to his full potential and to do even better at school.

During the short conversations with Max's teachers I became aware that I knew nothing about his school work and assignments as a consequence of my retreat into silence over the past year because I wanted to avoid another argument with him. I became aware that I had let my son down showing little interest what he was doing at school. That afternoon, I made a decision to change our relationship for the better even if it would be uncomfortable and challenging.

I started telling Karina that I had made a big step forward in the relationship with my Max having several short but meaningful conversations with him. I asked him about his feelings, a novelty in our household. The conversations were short, but I felt already that we were moving closer together after more than 12 months of silence.

Karina introduced the new work modality for the next weeks. Based on my questionnaire, we would start with the people who had been most influential in my life. With each person, we would go through a specific process of naming the feelings that this person triggered in me and then work through these feelings to clear them once for all. This would involve me having conversations with these people while calling them into the room and visualising them talking to me.

***

In one of our next sessions, I visualised my higher self-speaking with my husband's higher self. Karina encouraged me to open the conversation with whatever came to my mind. Without hesitation, I chose the events at the retreat. I explained how all the events during the week had culminated in my spiritual awakening during my Kahuna massage and how I had never felt anything like it with him in the 20 years we had been living together. I also explained that this Kahuna massage had triggered a chain of events in the following weeks, which reinforced my decision to follow my heart on this new journey to myself. A journey that had started many years ago when I had left everything behind in my country of birth to move to a new country. A journey that had led me further and further away from the man I was married to.

I expressed with clarity and honesty that I felt empty and out of place in our marriage and that I was curious to learn how my husband felt, if he was happy in our marriage.

Karina asked me if there had been specific events in the past that I wanted to bring to my husband's attention.

I mentioned my first visit to his mother's home in Adelaide in 1995 and that I never made the effort to start another conversation with him or her to find out why I had felt so out of place in her home.

I also recalled 2010 when my husband had to work in the UK for most of the year and left me and the boys alone in Sydney for many weeks in a row often postponing his return dates with short notice. The short periods he would come home ended in chaos, as the daily routines I had established with the boys were turned upside down. One day, when I mentioned my husband in a conversation with my sons, Max replied: 'Why do you worry about Dad, he's never here anyway.'

Then, there was his accident in April 2010 during our short Easter holiday in the Philippines. One of my husband's friends had invited us to visit him and his family in Manila. We had agreed that he would only fly over from the UK if he would not have to return on Easter. We met at Singapore Airport where we boarded a connecting flight to Manila and arrived at the resort early in the morning after long hours of travel and changing planes twice. Martin looked tired and exhausted. In the first night, he passed out while in the bathroom and fell hitting his head on the edge of the marble vanity. I was scared to death when I had found him lying on the floor his head bleeding. We ended up in a local hospital for the rest of the weekend. His friend and I asked him to stay with us for the rest of the week in their house in Manila to recover from his accident and let the wound heal. I was furious and felt disrespected when Martin turned down his offer and boarded his plane to the UK the next day.

And so the years went by with more unresolved issues piling up.

I became more and more aware that the lack of meaningful conversations and clear boundaries for many years was the main reasons for misunderstandings and frustration in our relationship and family. And I knew that it would be my responsibility to make the first step to seek a conversation with my husband about my emotions. I trusted in the Universe to tell me when the time had come.

Eventually, we went through a final clearing of all the negative feelings I had suppressed and carried with me for many years. When we finished, I found myself in a state of relief and heard Max say to me: 'It'll be ok, Mum.'

I opened our next session with the story of a woman I had met at a networking meeting. She had spent 15 months living and travelling in Europe with her family. They had sold their large property in Sydney, de-cluttered their furniture and possessions because they knew that after their return they would not be able to slip back into their 'old' life. They chose a very simple lifestyle while away. She explained to me that their choice of simplicity reframed their life and set the foundation for a simpler coastal lifestyle after their return to Australia. She was also able to find back to herself and define what was important to her and what freedom meant to her. After her return, she started coaching other women to find their freedom.

Her story resonated very much with me. During the past weeks, I questioned more and more often if I needed to live in a 5-bedroom house with multiple outdoor spaces and a swimming pool. The constant work around the house became a burden. When I was in the car, I realised how much time I had spent in the past eight years sitting in traffic jams. I started imagining how it would be to live outside the big city, surrounded by nature and little charming villages, driving on less congested roads, shopping in local shops or markets, living a more relaxed lifestyle.

Karina replied that she could see several themes in my stories I had told her since we met and encouraged me to explore each theme in isolation to find out what it meant to me or why it was important. The themes we defined were:

- Going away, travelling, spending time by myself
- Nature as a source of inspiration
- De-cluttering, letting go of physical and mental stuff

I liked the idea of exploring, lingering, wandering and wondering. I came to the realisation that I didn't know what my new normal would look like. Since returning from the retreat in January nothing was like it used to be.

At the end of our session, Karina asked me to choose two feathers from a selection of ten she had laid out on the floor. I love feathers and have many displayed around my home. The first one I chose was about 15 centimetres long, dark brown with four rows of little white spots on each side of the quill.

Karina picked it up and turned it around with her fingers.

'Why did you chose this one,' she wanted to know, 'what do you like about it, and what does it represent to you?'

I inspected the feather more closely and replied that I loved the details of the tiny white dots lined up in four rows parallel to the quill from the bottom to the top.

'The dots remind me of the labyrinth around the Buddha statue at the top of the retreat, overlooking the beautiful landscape. The path leads you in circles towards the Buddha in the centre. It's a journey of exploration and discovery, a walking meditation.'

'Beautiful,' Karina said, 'if I may add something, I would say that the lines of dots represent the layers of resources that are available to you on your journey.'

Then we looked at the second feather. It was a smaller feather with a very distinctive design: the bottom feathers created a contrasting pattern of a black and white landscape – with peaks and valleys similar to the drawings of a seismograph – then, completely unexpected, the feather became narrower and changed into an earthy red, very delicate, long tail, cheekily waving in the air if you shook the quill slightly.

'I was instantly attracted to the colour of the delicate tail, which represents a surprise, an unexpected detail in the overall design of this object,' I explained. 'I wonder from which bird it comes.'

Towards the end of our session, Karina asked if I had had more conversations with my son. When I said that I hadn't, she encouraged me to ask him how he would feel about having his German friend visiting for three months. We had spoken about the two of us needing our privacy and space to breathe.

ACCEPTANCE AND NON-ATTACHMENT

Surrender

"Peace begins when expectations end."

Sri Chinmoy, Indian Spiritual Leader

*****

Finally, the day had come. It was Friday, the 12th of May 2017, and my flight to Ballina was scheduled for 10am. I was in exceptionally good mood in anticipation of three days of pampering myself at the retreat. Six weeks, I had been looking forward to this day. Everything went to plan, and I arrived before lunch time at Ballina airport where a driver from the resort would pick me up. Not long and we passed the big iron gate to the retreat. I smiled silently when I saw the familiar sign "Your journey starts here".

In Kukura House, the main building of the retreat, the reception manager greeted me for check-in to one of the beautiful terraces with an outdoor deck and daybed. We chatted for a while about life in general, our children and the fact that mine were now old enough for me to be able to spend a weekend away. I told her how much I loved the Byron Bay hinterland since I had discovered it in 2009.

'We love to have you here,' she said, 'you have such a beautiful energy.'

It almost felt like coming home; being welcomed by old friends, who are very close to my heart. Not long after, one of the restaurant staff, approached me:

'Hi, Bettina, is it?'

'Hi, yes, I can't believe that you remember my name!' I was surprised.

'I'll show you your room,' she smiled and asked me to follow her.

Shortly after, I returned for lunch. Then, I strolled down to the spa where I was booked for a wellness consultation. In front of the spa building I ran into the General Manager.

'Welcome back! How are you?' he greeted me with a big smile and even bigger hug.

'Good, thanks.'

'You look great! When was the last time you were here?'

'Five months ago, after Christmas last year,' I replied. 'It was a very special visit. You wouldn't believe what happened after my Kahuna massage,' I heard myself say. 'It was life-changing.'

'Let's have a chat and catch up.'

'Yeah, I'd love to do that.'

'I'll let you know when I'm free.'

'Great, I'll wait to hear from you.'

I followed the naturopath to a quiet area near the pool where we sat down for half hour to talk about my general health and nutrition. Afterwards, I entered the spa reception to ask if, by any chance, there would be a massage available this afternoon.

'Hi Bettina, welcome back! Good to see you again,' Sonja, the spa manager, exclaimed when she saw me.

'Thanks. I just arrived and thought I'd see if there is someone available this afternoon for a relaxation massage.'

'Let me have a look, yes, we could do 3:30 if that suits.'

'Wonderful.'

I went back to my room, unpacked some clothes and checked my emails. Ten minutes prior to my treatment, I entered the spa complex.

Sonja approached me straight away.

'I'm so sorry, Bettina, Jay called in sick for tomorrow.'

She must have seen the shock in my face when I heard the devastating news.

'I know, it's a bummer. But I have one of our female therapists for you, if that's ok. She is great as well.'

'Oh, yes that's fine, whoever is available.' I forced myself to stay calm and not let my inner turmoil burst to the outside. I didn't want to believe what I just had heard; it couldn't be possible.

Six weeks I had been looking forward to this moment when I would meet Jay again. I wanted to share my story with him. In the meantime, my therapist for the afternoon had appeared and introduced herself. Like a robot, I followed her in one of the treatment rooms. My mind kept repeating the same question over and over again. What message was the Universe sending me? Then, I remembered my previous coaching session with Karina, when we had spoken about my upcoming weekend away. I had said to her that I hoped nothing would come in the way and that Jay would hopefully not be sick on that day. It was myself who had provoked this self-fulfilling prophecy!

I couldn't stop my mind from replaying the conversation at the reception. The chatter was so overpowering that I couldn't relax at all. After the massage, I sat outside in the same spot as five months ago, reminiscing the beautiful experience I had had on New Year's Eve and the priceless gift Jay had given me. I remembered the heightened sense of beauty that made me cherish everything around me. I remembered that I didn't want to share it with anyone but keep it in my heart, how I had felt energised and peaceful at the same time.

This Mother's Day, my heart was heavy, and it hurt digesting the bad news. I wandered back to my room where I collapsed on the bed, sobbing. I tried to make sense of the events in the past couple of hours. The Universe had sent me many messages in the past five months, all aligned with my journey. I knew that nothing happened without a reason. What message was the Universe sending me that day? Accepting that I would return to Sydney without being able to share my story with him was painful and hard to digest.

To distract myself from the unchangeable, I immersed myself into a pile of documents I wanted to read. A week before, I had started an online business in the health and wellness industry, becoming a brand partner with Arbonne. Arbonne is an international skincare company, that promotes a holistic approach to living and ageing well, with products and programs that embrace the Mind, Body, Skin connection.

The thought of having to survive financially on my own still freaked me out and this opportunity to earn some extra money, alongside my content writing work, had found me at the right time.

I sent a text message to the manager that I would love to meet him for a cup of tea on Sunday afternoon to let him know what happened since my last visit. The next day, we met after lunch at the library and I told him how Jay had turned my life upside with his massage on New Year's Eve.

'I'll let him know that you were here,' he said. 'But why don't you leave him a note and tell him that you would like to share your experience with him?'

I had thought about this before but was hesitant, as I was not sure whether this was an appropriate thing to do. We kept on chatting for an hour about the power of massages, how I had reconnected with my innermost self, the importance of following your intuition and how the Universe was offering us guidance if we are ready to hear it. I also mentioned that I felt drawn to the area around Byron Bay because, to me, it fostered creativity and radiated some kind of a healing vibe. The Manager nodded, 'I know what you mean.'

The next morning, the sun was shining and I spent a moment before my farewell breakfast sitting on one of the day beds on the property soaking in the beautiful scenery of the Byron Bay hinterland. The sunshine caressed my skin. I felt happy. I would love to live here, I thought.

As he had promised, the manager was in Kukura House to say goodbye. We hugged each other and he wished me well until we would see us again.

'Please let Jay know that I was here this weekend,' I reminded him of our conversation from the day before.

'I surely will.'

Back in my room, I got ready for departure, packed the last items in my suitcase and sat down at the timber desk. Once I had put the first words to paper, my pen danced across the page, and the words just seemed to flow out of it. I expressed my sadness that he was sick and my disappointed that I didn't have the chance to share my story with him. I also wrote that he would always have a very special place in my heart and thanked him for the priceless gift he had given me on the last day of 2016. I folded the paper and put it in an envelope which I handed over to one of the reception staff. The airport transfer was waiting for me.

A few days later, I looked up the quote on the 3rd of April in my Everyday Mindfulness guide. It was the day I had booked my weekend at the retreat:

"Peace begins when expectations end."

WHEN THINGS FALL APART

"Things falling apart is a kind of testing and also a kind of healing."

Pema Chödrön, Buddhist Nun, When Things Fall Apart

*****

On the 31st May, exactly five months after I had met Jay, I received an email from him with the subject line 'Many Thanks'.

He expressed his gratitude for my feedback and the heart-felt story I had shared in my note to him. He also wrote that he was still often moved by the power of his bodywork and to meet another person in such a sacred space. His message ended with the following wish: "May all our self-imposed barriers dissolve, and may this continue always." I read the five lines over and over again while my eyes filled with tears.

The first weekend in June was a big one with the launch of my online business. My business partner Marcia joined me to run the presentations and provide training on the products, the company and general administration tasks. The next milestone would be our training conference at the Gold Coast mid-September after which I planned to have another short break at the retreat. I couldn't wait to get there. Would I eventually meet Jay again?

I felt that the time had come to share my choice of leaving our marriage with more people. I hadn't spoken to my best friend from high school for a while. She lived in Germany and had no idea of my inner turmoil. I sent her a text message and we arranged a time to chat on the following weekend.

'Hi Ulli, I have something to tell you; it might be a shocker, but I'm going to separate from my husband.'

'What, why?' she exclaimed and I could almost see her face in disbelief at the other side of the world.

'That's a long story.'

'Well, then we'll have to make the time for it,' she replied.

In the next two and a half hours, as in the good old times when we were teenagers, I poured out my heart to her. She listened to me compassionately and at some point expressed her admiration:

'You are very brave and strong, and from what I hear from you, it seems to be the right decision.'

Again I felt this immense gratitude for my female friends who without hesitation offered me their help when they learned about my situation. Following Karina's advice, I only shared my story when it felt right and with people who had earned my trust. The more I practised listening to my body, the better I became in deciding what to do. I also noticed that since I had made the conscious decision after the Menstruation & Menopause workshop to care for my body and to listen to it more carefully, I had developed a heightened sense of body awareness and picked up its messages much quicker.

Mid-June we had our first reunion with the women of the Menstruation & Menopause workshop. I was still unsure if I should share what had happened in the meantime in my private life. I had briefly mentioned that I was working with a coach and that I went through a challenging phase in my marriage. When Katie, the workshop facilitator, greeted me that night and asked how I was going, the words came out of my mouth:

'Unfortunately, my marriage is coming to an end. I can't keep pretending to be the happy wife, especially not to my family and closest friends. The ongoing lack of communication from both of us over many, many years combined with too many suppressed emotions and my personal journey since we moved to Australia led me to make this decision. Our workshop opened my eyes to how much I had disregarded my body over the years'

'I thought that this might happen,' Katie said quietly.

We stood in the kitchen for quite a while, talking, and I felt a relief to be able to share my feelings with her.

In the following week, my body signalled that it was time to take the next step and talk to our sons. For more than four weeks I had slept in the guest room and none of them had come back to me with any questions. However, I was well aware of Max's ability to sense any upcoming changes and that he was watching. I remembered how he had picked up, when he was only six years old, that we were going to move to Australia. I mentioned my feeling with Karina and she only replied: 'You know what to do.'

To reveal my decision to my sons was challenging. A friend of mine had warned me that often the children thought that it was their fault that the parents wanted to separate. She suggested to make it very clear in our conversation that it was not, and that we both, my husband and I, would keep looking after them in our own way. Only the thought about this conversation made me feel sick. I finished my yoga practise every single time with a prayer to God and the Universe to give me the strength and wisdom to stay true to myself without hurting the people I love. My experiences in the past five months had repeatedly proofed that the only way to cope with upcoming challenges was to make one step at a time and to live day-by-day focusing on the present moment instead of worrying about the future.

My husband's behaviour at home exacerbated the situation. He kept calling me sweet names and wandered through the house whistling. We had a couple of conversations where I tried to find the right words to explain why I wanted to separate after 23 years. I described how the move to Australia and what I had experienced in the past ten years had changed me. I had left everything behind that meant something to me: my family, my career, my friends, our beautiful house. I started a new chapter of my life in a country that I only knew as a tourist.

I felt at the time that it was an opportunity to follow my creative calling finally. I always wanted to explore more creative work. When the opportunity to study interior design came up, I jumped in with both feet. I discovered my love for Street Latin dancing and started writing about my life connecting with creative communities in Sydney. I also committed to a regular yoga practice. I learned how to meditate and immersed myself in the Buddhist philosophy of life, which had caught my interest because of my yoga practice.

One thing led to another, and without realising it first, I moved away from my husband one step at a time. We seemed to travel in different directions. And the distance between us grew wider and wider as the years went by. I connected more and more with my spirituality which seemed a foreign territory for him.

'I am not the same person anymore who boarded that plane to Australia with you in 2008,' I tried to bring home my point. It almost felt like I was speaking in another language. Describing what I had experienced during my Kahuna massage was out of question.

I also found it increasingly awkward not to let our friends in on what was happening. We had been invited to a farewell party of one of my younger son's classmates, who was about to move back to Germany with his family. As we both knew the parents, we went to this party together, although I had made the decision to not accompany my husband to any events where we would appear as the happily married couple. At this party, I felt like exploring new territory. I avoided standing in the same group of people with him, and he seemed to do the same.

By now it dawned on me that I was the one in charge of driving the process, and I made an appointment for an initial consultation with a family lawyer who was highly recommended to me by one of my friends. I knew I needed a professional to help me, and it was important to me to find the right person. Someone I could trust.

A week later, I drove to the city for my first meeting with him. His assistant asked me to wait in one of his meeting rooms. I sat down and took a few deep breaths to calm myself. I felt slightly nervous, as I had never before dealt with a family lawyer, let alone talked to one about separating from my husband. Following my mantra 'You never have a second chance to make a first impression' I had chosen a business-like outfit with dark pants and an elegant blouse.

The moment he opened the door and greeted me with a firm hand shake and a broad smile, I knew that I had made the right decision. The following two-hour conversation reinforced my initial gut feeling. He listened to my case with compassion, instantly understood my situation and provided helpful advice. He also confirmed all the steps the lawyer at the council had explained to me. He spoke very openly about what I could expect and the challenges that might arise in the phase of transition into a new chapter of my new life. I left his office with the positive feeling that the Universe had again sent me the right person at the right time.

INFINITE POSSIBILITIES

"As the ego is no longer running your life, you are able to live with uncertainty, even enjoy it. When you become comfortable with uncertainty, infinite possibilities open up."

Eckart Tolle, A New Earth

*****

Early July, we had another conversation over dinner and I told my husband that I now wanted to let the boys in on what was happening. I suggested to talk to them the following Sunday. That was easier said than done. The Sunday came and I knew I couldn't do it that day. I felt unprepared and insecure.

'Didn't we want to talk to the boys today?' My husband asked in the afternoon.

'Yes,' I replied, 'but I don't know how to start. I can't do it today.'

'Yes, it's hard,' he concluded our short conversation.

That evening, I texted Karina to ask for another appointment to work out the approach for one the most difficult conversations in my life.

As always, I could count on her. She gave me valuable advice on how to structure this conversation and example phrases I could use to make my points. Afterwards, I wrote down a couple of pages as a guideline not to forget what I wanted to convey. The next day, I handed the paper to my husband to seek his opinion and approval.

At the end of the week, we agreed on the Saturday morning to talk to our sons after I would return from my morning yoga class where the Universe sent me another message. Our teacher spoke about vulnerability and encouraged us "to be vulnerable and show our emotions, otherwise we lose the connection to the world around us."

His words were still ringing in my ears when, an hour later, I called the boys in the living room.

'What do you want, Mum?' Max asked with impatience, not wanting to interrupt his computer game.

'Why do we need to come into the living room now?' Valentin wanted to know with a fearful tone in his voice. Having a family conversation in the living room was something out of their comfort zone, something that didn't happen very often.

'Please come into the living room,' I insisted, 'Dad and I need to talk to you.'

With a heavy heart, my cup of tea in one hand, my paper in the other, I sat down on a footstool in front of the lounge. My husband used the other foot stool, Max threw himself onto the lounge, and Valentin kept standing in front of the fireplace.

'Are we having a family assembly?' Max tried to smooth over his discomfort.

'You know that I moved into the guest room eight weeks ago,' I opened the conversation. 'The reason I did this was that I needed to become clearer about a few things, especially the relationship with Dad and how I want to live in the future. I've been suppressing many emotions in the past years and have come to the conclusion that I can't live like this any longer and will separate from Dad.'

I tried to look into my sons' eyes, which was a challenge as they were sitting and standing on either side of me. Max stayed calm and composed as I had anticipated, but his younger brother couldn't stop his tears after I had revealed the shocking news. I asked him to come and sit on my lap, which he followed promptly clinging onto me like a baby chimpanzee holding tight to his mother. He couldn't stop crying for a while, and I held him silently, tears running over my cheeks. No one spoke for what seemed to be an eternity, and I didn't interrupt the silence.

Then, my husband spoke, very calm and contained. He confirmed that we would both be looking after them and always be there for them; that they would have two homes in the future and, most importantly, that this decision had nothing to do with them.

When I looked at him, I saw a sad face. His emotions seemed to be trapped behind a heavy armour. I felt sorry for him.

I repeated that my decision was based on the fact that I had suppressed too many emotions in the past and that I could no longer keep pretending to be the happy wife; not to myself, not to them and not to all our friends.

Max looked at me, unmoved. 'Mum, I knew that this was coming.'

I was not surprised knowing my son's sixth sense.

'I remember that argument you had in January, when you left the dinner table one night,' he continued. 'And then, a few weeks later, can't remember when that was exactly, you came into my room, I was playing Lego, and you told me why you left that night. Then, when you moved into the guest room, I was wondering why.'

'Why did you never come to me and ask?' I wanted to know.

'I thought you would tell us someday.'

My son's answer proved again how uncommon the simplest conversations were in our family. I made it clear that I wished we would talk more often in the future, no matter what. I insisted that they could come to me any time and that there would be nothing that couldn't be sorted out.

At some point, Valentin got up from my lap and disappeared without a word into the family room to resume his online game.

I snuggled onto the sofa next to my teenage son and couldn't help the tears. I kept holding him with my head on his shoulder for a while. He didn't move. When I stopped crying, we started talking and I told him how proud I was of him. He asked a few questions about the future, where I would be living and if I could move closer to his school. We then talked about his school and his report and he finally opened up and told me some of the things that occupied his mind. I felt so grateful and relieved. This was the first real conversation with him since we had returned from Noosa three months ago.

We kept sitting on the sofa for about an hour, and I felt that this difficult conversation had opened infinite possibilities to a much better future for the entire family, even if we would not live together any longer.

After we had informed our sons, we could finally talk openly about the upcoming change. I felt relief and pride that I had initiated what had been the most difficult conversation in my life so far.

The boys adapted in their way. They didn't talk a lot about it, but from time to time a question or thought would come up. One night, at the dinner table, Valentin asked out of the blue how many beds we would have in my new home.

'Three,' I replied with a smile on my face, 'one for you, one for Max and one for me.'

'Good,' was all he said.

Another time, Max in his usual pragmatic approach, mentioned that he didn't like the fact that he would have to carry around his stuff every week from one house to the other. A couple of weeks after we spoke to them, I addressed both of them separately to ask if any questions had come up for them in the meantime.

'Mmh, no, I actually haven't been thinking about it anymore,' Max said confirming my assumption how he would deal with the situation until the separation would actually become reality. There were obviously too many other things that occupied the mind of a 15-year-old teenager.

LOVE WHERE YOU ARE GOING

"The spiritual journey involves going behind hope and fear, stepping into the unknown territory, continually moving forward."

Pema Chödrön, Buddhist Nun

*****

The first half of 2017 had come to an end. The new normal was to live separated from my husband under the same roof. Sometimes, I wondered how I had managed to get through the weeks and months living in uncertainty every single day. The direction of my journey had become clearer, but the destination was not in sight yet. Another card reading revealed "the end of an era" and "a cycle of beginnings and endings".

Some days were easy, some difficult. I didn't sleep very well and woke up regularly from unsettling nightmares. Often, my husband, family members and old friends from Germany were the protagonists. I tried to stay detached, find the space between pleasure and pain, between hope and fear, between desperation and excitement. A constant challenge. On the difficult days, I felt exhausted and my body answered with the habitual tightness in my stomach, which left me without appetite. Then, there were the days when I felt uplifted and empowered, knowing that it would all work out, that there was a reason why I was going through this change. I often found solace in my books, such as Marcus Aurelius' Meditations where he wrote that the strands of fate and what happens to us has been connected since the beginning of time.

I didn't know how to cope without writing. My journal had become a close friend who I could tell everything when I felt like it, any time of the day. On some days, my pen flew over the lined pages to record a win, a success, a positive feeling. Sometimes, I only documented snippets of thoughts, an idea or inspirational quote or something I might do. Sometimes I just vomited my thoughts and complaints on the paper, it was my way of getting the stuff out of my head and telling it to someone imaginary. I also documented all the dreams I could remember. I tried to look forward and to stay positive. I often looked at my new vision board, a daily reminder, for the next 18 months: "No looking back. Love where you're going.'

Although the calendar said we were still in winter and the morning hours were cold and chilly, spring announced itself with balmy days and lots of sunshine to brighten up my mind. It was now mid-August and I had to come to terms with the fact that 'nothing goes quickly in family law land,' as my lawyer repeatedly pointed out to me when I got impatient with the process of our property settlement.

I often turned to my Butterfly Cards for Life Changes and, as if to confirm what I knew already, I drew the card Self-Care. "This card is asking you to retreat for some much needed rest and self-care." By now, I had learned how important it was that I looked after myself. I found ongoing support in my almost daily yoga practice and was looking forward to mid-September when I would return to the Byron Bay hinterland.

The same night, I received the next message from the Universe. I attended a monthly women's circle, facilitated by my coach. We talked about boundaries, what they mean to us, how we set them and keep them in place in challenging times. As the group was only small that night, we gathered around a square bar table decorated with tea lights and several decks of cards. To begin, we drew cards from all the decks and laid them out in front of us. I started with the Angel cards.

When I turned my card around, I saw Archangel Michael, the epitome of strength and courage, the most powerful of all the angels. This was the fourth time that he appeared in my life in the past 18 months. As "he is considered a leader within the angelic realm and a patron angel of righteousness, mercy and justice," he is often depicted as a warrior with sword in his hand. He is also known for supporting us in life changes.

The next day, I started emptying the bookshelf in the living area and removed all the artworks from the walls, as we had decided to repaint the living and dining room as well as the kitchen before putting our house on the market for sale. Within a couple of hours, the room became half empty. Although I knew I would decorate the shelf again afterwards, it felt like moving out already. I decided to de-clutter some of my books and CDs. The less stuff I would have to move, the easier it would be. I couldn't help thinking of the moment we closed the front door of our house in Wiesbaden for the last time nine years ago. Images of us standing next to the truck and looking back at an empty shell, a home that had lost its soul. Another lump started to form in my stomach and I forced myself to concentrate on the here and now. I hoped that I would be able to take this new bookshelf, which we had only bought a couple of years before, and which held my treasured collection of books, keepsakes, and photos; things that reminded me of many happy times in my life. And Martin had already agreed that I could have it.

The new chapter of my life started to take form with Archangel Michael leading the way.

YOU ARE NOT YOUR BODY

"Love is the energy that silently transfigures every situation."

David R. Hawkins, Power vs Force

*****

In early September, I decided to inform my sons' teachers about our separation. As I had expected, they were supportive and compassionate. We agreed that they would not tell the boys that I had spoken to them but just watch them. We also agreed to seek parenting mediation to find the best solution for to look after our sons in the future.

Finally, things seemed to move in the right direction, and I was so looking forward to my upcoming trip to the Gold Coast.

On Friday, the 8th of September, life threw me in the middle of the next fire. It was the end of another emotionally strenuous week. The last task for the day was to cook dinner. Reluctantly, I gathered the ingredients I needed. I never liked cooking very much, and it was the last thing I wanted to do that evening. I started cutting the vegetables and grating the cheese for the baked dish. The Parmesan cheese was a particularly hard block, and I had to push firmly on the grater. Halfway through, I changed the position of the blade to get some thicker slices and kept going. Next, the remaining block of the cheese broke in two, and my right thumb landed on the blade of the grater. It all happened within a flash of a second; the blade chopped off the edge of my thumb, and I stared at a big hole, which instantly filled with blood bubbling out of my finger. I didn't feel any pain in this very moment and turned around the grater to find the missing piece of my thumb underneath. More and more blood streamed out of my finger, and I grabbed a large piece of the paper towel that stood right in front of me.

'Max, I need your help!' I shouted into the adjacent family room where the boys were immersed in their computer games, headphones on. As there was no reaction, I opened the sliding door and repeated my command. When my 15-year-old saw the bloody paper towel I was pressing on my finger, he finally got up. I instructed him to get the first aid kit and put a pressure bandage around my finger.

'Mum, you better go to the hospital,' was his only comment.

Luckily, my husband was on his way home and only ten minutes away. When he arrived, I jumped straight into his car, and we drove to the local hospital. In the meantime, the initial shock, which had numbed all pain, had faded and I concentrated on breathing through the throbbing pain in my right hand. It seemed like an eternity until the car finally stopped in front of the emergency entrance. I hated the old, dilapidated complex and remembered the year before where I spent several hours with Martin inside its walls when he had dislocated his shoulder.

As expected there were other people sitting in the grim waiting room, and after checking in, a nurse looked at the wound, which was excruciatingly painful, and wrapped my bleeding finger up again.

'Have a seat in the waiting room until a doctor has time to look after you,' she advised us with a friendly but firm tone and handed me a couple of pain killers. Reluctantly, I sat down and tried to keep my arm up to reduce the pain of my throbbing thumb. The pain seemed to spread over my whole body. It took almost an hour until we were finally asked by a female doctor to follow her in one of the treatment rooms. There, the pain escalated to new heights when she unwrapped my thumb and applied pressure to the wound to stop the bleeding. Over the course of the following four hours, they ran out of ideas how to stop the blood flowing. I was pumped up with pain killers and antibiotics and felt more and more weakened, losing control over my trembling body, almost fainting.

At some point, they gave me a zipper bag full of ice cubes to press around my hurting finger. After a while, both of my hands felt half frozen and numb. However, it seemed that the blood flow had slowed down slightly. There was nothing else to do than to wait and hope that it would stop. Otherwise, they would not let me go home. In between changing the bandages, which almost made me faint because of the pain level I had to cope with, they tried to take several pictures for the plastic surgeon – another excruciating exercise, as they had to push hard on the wound to stop the blood for a millisecond to get the right shot.

I prayed to Heaven and the Universe that I would not have to spend the night in the emergency ward. The Gods must have heard my plea, as shortly before midnight, the blood slowed down to an extent where they agreed to let me go home with the premise to return at 8 am the next morning to see the surgeon. Before I left, they put a needle in my left hand, gave me an intravenous injection of antibiotics and forbid me to eat anything until the surgeon had seen the wound in the morning. There was a potential skin graft operation looming on the horizon.

Needless to say that I didn't get a lot of sleep that night. With my right hand in a vertical position leaning at a couple of cushions and an infusion needle stuck in the left hand, I lay immobile on my back and counted the hours until I would have to return to the hospital.

At 8 am, we were checking in again only to find that no one was there to look after me. After another hour in the uncomfortable waiting room, I felt more and more dizzy with no food in my stomach since 4 pm the previous afternoon. My right shoulder and arm were hurting from the constant effort to keep the hand in a lifted position above my heart.

It must have been 9:15 am when the ward door opened and a young Asian woman in a casual outfit, jeans and jumper, asked me to follow her. The pain was almost unbearable when she took off the bandage and more photos of my still bleeding thumb.

After wrapping my thumb up again, she disappeared telling me that she would get back to us within an hour with the final decision about what to do next. I was wondering who she was, as she didn't seem to find it necessary to introduce herself.

I asked to lie down in the small rectangular treatment room, as I felt weaker and weaker and was again on the brink of losing consciousness What I understood was that the hand plastic surgeon, who would make the final decision about how to continue the treatment, was working in the operating theatre. I lost track of time and fell in a half sleep. Suddenly, one of the nurses appeared with a sandwich and a cup of tea and left without further explanations. I was relieved that I could finally eat something and that the operation had obviously been cancelled.

It was almost lunch time, and my husband had to leave to get some of the Saturday chores done. While he was away, I surrendered to my destiny and lay back down in the treatment room. A while later, another nurse appeared to transfer me to the transit ward where she accompanied me in an abandoned room at the end of a corridor. It was furnished with random chairs, tables, and empty beds. I sat down in one of the chairs amidst the other furniture pieces my right hand attached to a sling to keep it vertical and to reduce the pain. I merged seamlessly with the leftover furniture that didn't fit anywhere else and started wondering if anyone would find me here. Another two hours passed; the silence interrupted from time to time with a nurse coming in to measure my blood pressure and temperature or to ask if I needed anything. My questions about when the surgeon would come back remained unanswered. Eventually, she arrived, changed my bandage one last time and sent me home with the recommendation to make an appointment with a hand plastic surgeon three days later. When we came home that afternoon, after eleven hours in the emergency ward, I was so exhausted that I slept for most of the weekend.

In the following days, I read in Louise Hay's bestseller Heal Your Body that the thumb represents the intellect and worry. I was forced to use my left hand for the majority of the time and the most mundane tasks such as brushing my teeth or closing the zipper of my pants became a challenge. I had to concentrate and think about actions that I would normally perform mechanically and unconsciously. Weeks later, when I finally was able to go back to my yoga classes with my thumb still bandaged, Keenan asked me what had happened. When I told him that I had cut off a part of my thumb, he smiled at me and said: 'You are not your body.' Totally surprised about this reaction, I didn't say anything but kept thinking about his answer for days.

Although my thumb was still bandaged and I couldn't use my right hand properly, I attended my first Arbonne National Training Conference at the Gold Coast with more than 2,500 consultants from Australia and New Zealand. The 3-day training filled with personal development, hands-on product training, and invaluable community connection was mind-blowing in many ways. It was mind-blowing in many ways. My biggest takeaway was a simple question that one of our international keynote speakers raised: Whose day did you make today? She shared a story of her experiences with her children, who never talked a lot when she asked them how their day had been. One morning, she decided to change her question and asked them to tell her every day after school whose day they had made that day. This question changed the entire conversation and had become their mantra to the extent that they reminded each other 'to make someone's day today' when they left the house in the morning.

I loved this story and introduced this question to my sons after my return. Max looked at me as if I had completely lost the plot and didn't say a lot, as usual. However, Valentin, embraced the challenge and started telling me little things he had done to make someone else happy. One day, he returned from school and told me excitedly that he had shared his lunch with his classmate. Another day, he helped me washing the dishes after my traumatic accident.

I also had a lightbulb moment on the second day of the conference. I woke up at 2:20 am with the sudden awareness that the reason why I had started my Arbonne business was to show my sons that they can rewrite their stories any time in their lives. At the same time, I found an explanation of what had happened during my Kahuna massage in David R. Hawkins' book Power vs Force. After 20 years of research about the energy fields of human levels of consciousness, he had developed a map of energy fields of consciousness, which he described as "the geography of man's experience."

As the author wrote "Truly spiritual states can be said to begin at a calibrated level of about 500 (Love), become Unconditional Love at 540, and then continue to infinity… It is not an uncommon experience for students to enter into such a sublime state when in the presence of teachers whose energy fields calibrate at 550 and over, through the process of 'entrainment,' which is the dominance of a powerful attractor field."

The author recounted his first spiritual experience as "a state of peace beyond all description." He further elaborated that this state was enhanced by "A presence of infinite love that had no beginning and no end and was undifferentiated from my own essence." He felt that his physical body and surroundings had blurred and he wrote: "My awareness was fused with this all-present, illuminated state. My mind had gone silent; all thought stopped."

I reread these paragraphs over and over again and realised that these words summed up perfectly what I had experienced during my Kahuna massage. I remembered the description in retreat's spa menu where Jay had written that the core of his bodywork was to give and to receive love. My wish to see him again was not granted, though. On the second day of our conference I received a call from the spa manager that Jay had reported sick that week. I had to accept that a reunion with him was not meant to be. I didn't need him anymore on my path forward. It was time to let go.

PARENTING MEDIATION

"Surrender to what is. Let go of what was. Have faith in what will be."

Sonia Ricotti, Leadership Coach and Author

*****

Early October, Unifam asked us for a joint appointment to discuss in detail how we both planned to manage our parenting duties in the future. We each raised our points and within two hours had put together the framework for our parenting plan. Again, the meeting had a business-style atmosphere with hardly any emotions. We left with a signed agreement that we wished the boys to be included in this process.

I was concerned about their emotional wellbeing. As usual, since they had learned about the separation, they hardly spoke about how they felt. I attempted several times to find out what occupied their mind with not much success. I hoped that talking to professional mediators would be helpful for them to process this significant change in their life.

A couple of weeks later, each of our sons spent 45 minutes with one of Unifam's child mediators. Neither Max, nor Valentin revealed a word about what they had done, said, or heard in their session. And I didn't ask. However, I noticed my older son's appearance with slightly red cheeks and dishevelled hair. He seemed excited about the meeting and relieved at the same time. 'Oh man, I spoke the whole time,' was all he said. When we walked back to our car through pouring rain, he whistled cheerfully. I refrained from asking any questions, curiously awaiting our feedback session a couple of weeks later.

On the 31st October, Jenny welcomed us again into her office. For the third time, I took a seat around the small round table that stood in the middle of the room. My husband sat opposite me and Andy, the child mediator, between the two of us.

'Is there anything you want to say before Andy starts with his report?'

'Yes,' I said, 'I want to say something. I would like to thank you, Andy, for your time and work with our sons. Initially, they were not very happy when I told them that we would like them to see you. But when we went home that day, especially Max was in a very good mood and seemed so relieved that he could talk to someone other than his parents. So, thank you very much for your help.'

In the next 30 minutes, Andy went through his script and summarised the 90-min session with our sons. He had spoken to them separately, asked lots of questions and collected their feedback. He started acknowledging that both our sons had agreed that he could share anything they said. Some of the highlights were their descriptions of Mum and Dad and what they liked about us. I was again impressed by Max's fine antennas and his ability to pick up on subtle changes in the behaviour of the people around him. Although he didn't talk much and seemed quite retreated in his world, he was well aware of what was going on around him.

Overall, Andy praised the boys' ability to express themselves and articulate their opinion. He also confirmed that they seemed to cope quite well with the situation and that he couldn't see any warning signs for a critical condition. He handed us a one-page document with a list of suggestions how to deal with the crucial points regarding the parenting plan and how to move forward so that it would be in the best interest of the children. Additionally, he offered his help should we feel that it would be beneficial for the children to have other sessions with him in the future. I quite liked the idea and jotted a reminder in my notebook to reconnect with Andy in the future.

Finally, Jenny scheduled another mediation session to finalise the parenting plan. She asked us to review our minutes from the previous meeting and to consider the feedback from the children over the next couple of weeks.

After six months of living separated under the same roof while dealing with the lawyers, the situation at home became more and more tense. It became harder and harder to play my role as the happy wife, to keep myself together for the sake of no disputes in front of the boys. I felt liberated during the day when I was alone but then turned into a functioning robot when my husband returned home in the evening. My body made itself heard louder and louder. I had been dealing with a strange pain in my left foot for a couple of weeks, and my aggressive allergic cough had returned after years with many sleepless nights as a result.

*****

A few days later, I spoke to a girlfriend on the phone when she surprised me with some news:

'Did Valentin tell you about his conversation with Per and David at school yesterday?'

'No, what conversation?'

'Per told me that Valentin had revealed to him and another friend that his parents were going to separate in the beginning of the next year. When the boys asked him if he was sad, he said yes, he had been but that he felt better now,' my friend repeated her son's description of the event.

I was so happy to hear these words. The weekend before we had had a conversation with the boys to discuss how we thought we could go about the parenting plan. We presented them a couple of suggestions as an answer to their feedback we had received from the child mediator. The major concern of my older son was the week-about agreement, as he didn't like the idea of moving between houses every Friday after school.

My husband and I had discussed a few scenarios and asked the boys to join us to present them the solution we felt would work best. It was a casual chat and both Max and Valentin agreed on changing houses every fortnight on a Sunday afternoon rather than the Friday. I confirmed that I would organise a TV screen for Valentin, and Max was happy to move his computer every second week. I felt that the boys appreciated that they could have their say and were heard, and we all agreed that we would test our initial plan and adjust it after a few months if necessary. I was relieved and grateful that I had followed my lawyer's advice and insisted on the negotiations with Unifam. The following evening, Valentin and I were laying on my bed. He would often come in my room before he went to bed having a cuddle with me. We talked about the upcoming move.

'Mum, I'm now really excited about designing my room,' he suddenly said referring to our conversation the day before about which room each of the boys would get in their Dad's house. My heart jumped in my chest, as I knew how hard it would be for him to move out of our home in Clontarf, which he remembered as his family home. He was three when we moved into it and hardly remembered anything from his first years living in Germany.

'Yes, that's great,' I replied, 'and what's even better is that you get to design two rooms.'

FINDING SOLACE

"Hold the sadness and pain of Samsara in your heart and at the same time the power and vision of the Great Eastern Sun. Then, the warrior can make a proper cup of tea."

Trungpa Rinpoche, Tibetan Buddhist meditation master

*****

With yoga, meditation, and revisiting some of my Buddhist philosophy books I managed to get through the days. The writings of Pema Chödrön summed up my feelings pretty accurately:

"When you really start the warrior's journey – which is to say, when you start to want to live your life fully instead of opting for death, when you begin to feel this passion for life and for growth, when discovery and exploration and curiosity become your path – basically, if you follow your heart, you are going to find that it's often extremely inconvenient."

I had to face the harsh reality that I would have to cope with living another three to four months with my husband under the same roof. As so often in the past, I asked Karina for help.

'It's time to shine the torch back on you,' she suggested. 'You can't change the situation, so it's your choice whether you want to fight the reality or whether you concentrate on yourself, stand firm and set your boundaries for the next months. Forget about what was or how it used to be, create new rules and live by them.'

I loved her practical approach and made up my mind to work out some new rules around living together with my husband in the same house. My body started to rebel against the dreaded time when we would sit together at the table. My core tightened and didn't enjoy the food. Often, I wasn't even hungry. To make things worse, my allergic cough was very persistent.

By mid-November, I was looking forward to seeing my lawyer again after almost three months of phone and email communication. In those past weeks, although our correspondence obviously centred around family law, I got glimpses of him as a person outside his law firm and I liked what I had heard. We seemed to share similar interests.

I called him when I arrived outside his office. Not long and he appeared with a smile on his face. We walked side-by-side to a coffee shop around the corner. I enjoyed his presence, as he always made me feel safe and looked after. We spent an hour discussing the next steps to finally come to a conclusion of our case. I mentioned how much my almost daily yoga and meditation practise meant to me and that I found a lot of solace in the Buddhist philosophy of life.

'That's not for me,' I heard his voice with a slightly sad tone. 'I lost one of my best friends to Buddhism. He became a monk and now lives in a monastery in Western Australia.' At the same time, he had pulled out his mobile phone and showed me a picture of a young guy, dressed in the traditional orange clothing of Buddhist monks, sitting cross-legged in a meditation cave. I only had a short look at the image but could see an attractive young male with glaring blue eyes.

'He is here in Sydney at the moment, he has an event at Camperdown library tomorrow night,' he continued. 'You would love him, he's amazing.'

'I have other plans tomorrow, what a shame,' I replied, and we kept discussing family law matters. We agreed to send another letter communicating very clear boundaries including to respect my wish not to talk about financial things at home any more.

The next time, I spoke to my lawyer, I mentioned that I had looked up his friends Facebook page and that I was intrigued to meet him.

'He's still around,' I heard him say.

'You mean he is still in Sydney?'

'Yes, for quite some time.'

'Do you think I could meet him one day? Could you arrange this for me?' I hardly dared to ask what would mean the world to me.

'Yes, sure, happy to do this for you.'

'Oh my God, that would be awesome! I'd be forever grateful.'

One day, while I was waiting at the bus stop to pick up my son, I randomly browsed Facebook and came across another event held by my lawyer's Buddhist friend that night. I clicked on the Messaging tab and started typing. I wrote a short introduction how I had heard about him, that I had been practising yoga and meditation for seven years and that I would love to meet him before his return to Western Australia. Before I could think too long about what I was doing, I hit the 'send' button.

Within a minute, my phone announced the arrival of a new Facebook message with the well-known pinging sound. I couldn't believe my eyes; there was an answer from Buddhist monk, saying that had heard about me when they had lunch the other day and that he was happy to meet me. He finished with his encouragement to keep practising meditation, as the practice would add many benefits to my life and the life of others. I replied that I would be delighted to meet him.

The next day, I got a phone call from my lawyer, who was confident that we would resolve our case before Christmas. Before he could even say a word, I burst with excitement about the Facebook conversation I had the day before.

'Can you believe this? I messaged your friend yesterday and he replied within a minute! He is happy to meet me in January. He said that he might give another talk at the Buddhist Library and that we could catch up then. I am so excited!'

'That's great to hear, we spoke about you the other day. I might come with you, as I never go to these things,' he replied.

The following days, I kept reflecting on this new tribe of people that the Universe kept sending my way. It had all started with my Kahuna massage. Because of this unsettling experience, I had reconnected with Karina. In April, Arbonne found me, out of the blue when I was looking to earn some extra money. A month later, I had found the best family lawyer any woman could wish for. In November, a new financial adviser joined my support team. At the end of a challenging year, I had the pleasure to meet an ordained Buddhist monk who happened to be my lawyer's best friend.

The more I thought about what had happened in the course of the year and who I had met, the more I was certain that nothing was a coincidence and that all these people came into my life for a reason. Because I had put it out to the Universe that I was seeking for a specific person – I had placed orders in the Universal kitchen, as Louise Hay put it in her books – these people appeared when the time had come and I needed them to move forward on my new path. What I learned from this experience is that the more I surrendered to life and let go of any expectations, the easier it was to let these new people enter my life and connect with them. It required trust and faith that everything would work out in the end and that the right people would show up when I needed them.

I was curious how these relationships would unfold and who else would cross my path in the next twelve months.

CLEARING THE FOG

"When things are shaky and nothing is working, we might realise that we are on the verge of something."

Pema Chödrön

*****

'You need a break,' I heard my lawyer's firm voice at the other end of the line.

Following his suggestion to get out of the house, I was about to leave to Billabong Retreat for five days of solitude, rest, meditation, reflection, and writing. There was no doubt that I needed this time out.

'Go and have a rest for a few days, it won't make any difference. If I hear from your husband's lawyer, I'll ask him to prepare the papers. We've made our offer, he only needs to accept it,' he kept going, more talking to himself than to me.

'I'm so sick,' I confessed to him, 'this week, I now have a cold on top of the ongoing cough I've had for seven weeks now. Yesterday, I saw one of my yoga teachers who is also an acupuncturist and doctor in traditional Chinese medicine, and he confirmed that this cough is the result of emotional stress, that the lungs hold grief and that we would need to resolve the underlying emotions to get rid of the cough. I feel so depleted and drained, like a wreck, I have hardly any energy left.'

'I can hear that. That's why you need to go away and rest.'

Was this really my lawyer talking to me? He sounded more like a best friend worrying about my wellbeing. When I heard his voice on the phone, I instantly felt better regardless of what we were talking about. The week before I had told him that I wanted to give him a little present before he would close his office over Christmas and New Year. In my card, I had explained how much I valued his legal advice, support, and compassion and that I truly hoped we would stay friends in the future.

A few hours later, I sat in the car driving to Maraylya, a suburb in the vicinity of Rouse Hill and Windsor, in Sydney's northwest. I didn't feel well at all. As I listened to an album of Curtis Stigers and one of his hits from the early 90s, I Wonder Why, my eyes filled with tears and I kept sobbing while he sang "tears of frustration roll down my face."

I had heard of Billabong Retreat before but had not been aware that it was so close to Sydney. Once I turned off Old Windsor Road, I found myself in the countryside driving past large properties scattered in the landscape with large meadows with cows and horses in between. Several turns later, the streets got narrower, the forest denser, I almost missed the wooden sign 'Billabong Retreat' on my right. I steered my car along a gravel road through the dense forest towards the reception area. The check-in was done in a matter of minutes, and the young receptionist gave me a short tour around the communal areas including a dining room, a lounge room, the yoga studio above the wellness centre and the adjacent magnesium-enriched pool. She then directed me to the lodge, which was the original family home of the owner and had been transformed into a communal space with five bedrooms for guests. Here I would stay the first two nights before moving to one of their Tree House rooms for the rest of my stay.

The retreat offered a daily schedule that you could participate in or not including morning and afternoon yoga, guided mediation, and workshops around mindfulness. The one that had sparked my interest was called *Mindfulness Essentials* and focused on the science of neuroplasticity. I was looking forward to learn more about how we can refine the habitual patterns of the mind to improve function and abilities of the brain through regular brain training practice. The brochure promised stress reduction, increased resilience to conflict and change, more insight into the science of neuroplasticity and epigenetics, and tips to become happier, healthier, and more productive; it sounded as it was made for me.

I decided to take the first couple of days easy and to rest as much as I could. I skipped the Vinyasa yoga class on Saturday morning and sat down on the deck. The lodge was a perfect place to write. It had a large, covered timber veranda going around the house with a deeper deck at the back overlooking the billabong. The water looked like an oval-shaped mirror framed with rows and rows of round green leaves touching and overlaying each other. From this bed of leaves, flower stems, which reminded me of oversized matches, shot in the air. The buds were still closed, but one could spot hints of purple breaking through, and I hoped the flowers would open before I left. The next day, my wish was fulfilled and suddenly the frame of yellow-green was sprinkled with pink and purple water lilies opening up their bright yellow hearts and stretching to the sun.

The mornings were particularly beautiful. The air was fresh and crisp, little ducks made their rounds in the billabong leaving ripples of water behind them. There was an abundance of birds breaking the silence and peacefulness of the early morning hours. On the first day, I spotted a group of whip birds with their distinctive whoop sound on the nearby lawn. Another time, it was a couple of crimson rosellas with their bright red feathers who caught my attention. One evening, on my way back from the dining room to the lodge, I spotted a round spiky ball in the underwood; an echidna curled up next to a pile of wood logs. The folder in my room also listed finches, king parrots, black cockatoos, and kookaburras to look out for in the air. When I read about a two-metre long lace monitor which could be found hiding up in the trees, I was not so sure if I wanted to meet this wildlife species. Another guest, however, confirmed that she had seen one the other evening.

I treasured being in the midst of nature listening to the morning choir of the different birds, watching the ducklings following their mother around the billabong. One day I must have scared a wallaby who was hiding between the grass at the shore of the lake. I had spent some time meditating sitting on a grassy area next to him, not aware that he was there, and when I got up and walked around on the lawn, he suddenly jumped up and hopped away, startling me.

I enjoyed staying in the lodge away from the main building and most of the other accommodation. I very much enjoyed being by myself and the mere fact of being away from home lifted my spirits. It felt like a someone had taken a burden off my shoulders.

I eagerly awaited the mindfulness workshop with Paul van Bergen, founder of the retreat. It promised to be very captivating, and I was not disappointed. The topic was fascinating and a welcome distraction from my illness. In the first session, Paul introduced us to the history of yoga and meditation, which he explained as self-transformation through self-observation. His defined mindfulness as "paying attention, on purpose, in the present moment, without judgement." He went on to explain the structure of our brain and how we have the power, through a consistent meditation practice and becoming an observer of our mind and body, to activate both the right and left side of our brain. Through meditation, we become aware of our thoughts, words, worries, our external consciousness, which is our body in space, and our internal consciousness, our organs and internal systems that make the body function. Paul finished the first session reminding us of the infinite potential of our minds and that we have the choice to inhabit the most evolved part of our brain by practising conscious and mindful living.

Day two was all about the science behind mindfulness, and we heard about neuroplasticity, meta cognition, emotional intelligence, and epigenetics. From the thousands of studies done each year how mediation can impact our brain, Paul quoted one which had found enlarged parts of the prefrontal cortex in a group of people who meditated 30 minutes each day for eight weeks. We then looked at the path to turn unconscious bad habits into conscious bad habits, conscious good habits and eventually into unconscious good habits, which should become our default mode. Paul also mentioned the obstacles we have to overcome to find this clarity by consciously observing everything that happens to us. I particularly liked his metaphor that mindfulness means "clearing away the fog on the windows."

The more we practise mindfulness, the better we become at observing ourselves; our mind observing itself, when it is entangled in thoughts about the past and worries about the future instead of being in the present moment. To master the art of meta cognition makes you realise that you are neither your body nor your thoughts. At this point, I remembered the comment of one of my yoga teachers when I showed him my bandaged right thumb and told him that I had chopped off part of my finger. Keenan's first words were: "You are not your body." At the time, I was surprised about his reaction, now I understood what he had meant.

We also discussed stress versus mindfulness and how stress triggers a sympathetic response, whereas mindfulness, elicits a response from our parasympathetic nervous system. Finally, Paul touched on emotional intelligence and the fact that our thoughts and emotions are infinitely linked, which means that one triggers the other and vice versa. He encouraged us to use our emotions to guide us but not become a slave of them.

The last topic of day two was epigenetics and the discussion if our DNA and what we inherited from our parents controls our behaviour, or if the 50 trillion cells that our body is made of can be influenced by our thoughts and beliefs. A topic that captivated my mind, and I couldn't wait to read the book *The Biology of Belief* that I had discovered in a workshop about traditional Chinese medicine and yin yoga a couple of weeks before.

The third session focussed on practical tips how to apply mindfulness in our daily life at home and at work. Paul's summary of the most important takeaways from his workshop included the following tasks:

1. Anchor your day with a formal, personal practice in the morning.

2. Seek informal practice, for example, going to yoga classes on a regular basis

3. Avoid self-catastrophising.

4. Seek minute meditations throughout the day.

5. Review work before going home (and set yourself up for the next day).

6. Practice mindfulness before going to bed.

On my way home, I felt reassured that I was on the right path, a path I had been following for eleven months to steer my life into a different direction. However, the closer I approached the Northern Beaches, the bigger the tightness in my stomach grew. The days at billabong retreat had felt like living in a cocoon, protected and safe, far away from the ordeal I was going through at home.

CHRISTMAS 2017

"Grief is passive, a Yin movement of total surrender to nothingness."

Christine Li and Ulja Krautwald, The Path of the Empress

*****

After my return from the retreat, we were only one week away from the Christmas break, and I wondered if we could still come to an agreement before the end of the year.

As often these days, I turned to my card deck. I smiled when I drew the card GRIEF WORK. It signalled that my heart needed some healing from one or more losses and that this healing would be needed to move forward with my life. The card further confirmed that although mourning and crying might be uncomfortable, it is the only path to healing and that loss is painful but can help us develop compassion and greater appreciation of life.

Every night, I wrote down what occupied my mind. My journal had become my saviour, a trusted friend whom I poured out my heart as often and as long as I wanted. I knew I was on the home stretch with the settlement negotiations but it was rough territory I was walking on. One evening when I wrote down the events of the day, I suddenly felt a sense of calm emanating from my centre. The warrior is ready for the fight, I noted, firmly grounded on Mother Earth, her soft gaze straight ahead determined to follow her chosen path.

I met with my lawyer for breakfast a last time before the Christmas break. He greeted me with a broad smile on his face and a big hug:

'You've lost so much weight and look sick,' he said with a concerned tone in his voice.

As always in his presence I felt instantly better, and we walked side-by-side, chatting along, to the same café we had visited four weeks earlier. While eating our breakfast, we spoke about Christmas and my husband's upcoming trip with the boys to Adelaide. In between, we discussed how to best respond to my husband's last letter to eventually come to an agreement. We sat outside the café for over an hour and I still had not finished my breakfast. I had to force myself to eat at every meal, as my appetite seemed to have left me most of the time.

'I can't even eat this bowl of muesli,' I sighed.

'That's ok, at least, you've eaten half of it,'

When we said goodbye he gave me a big hug and wished me well.

'Just remain silent at home. Something will happen in the next days, and we'll speak before the end of the week.'

And so it happened. By the end of the week, we agreed on our property settlement.

I felt mentally exhausted and depleted with my ongoing sickness on top of the emotional rollercoaster during that week. In the afternoon, I sat outside on our deck and suddenly started crying. Tears of sadness rolled down my cheeks despite the fact that Martin and I had finally agreed on our property settlement. Instead of relief or happiness, all I could feel was this overpowering feeling of loneliness in every cell of my body. I felt the urge to leave the house and found myself at Manly Beach again. The afternoon sun was still shining, and I wore my sun glasses to cover my eyes which constantly filled with tears while I was walking bare foot along the edge of the water. I remembered Thich Nhat Hanh's instructions for walking meditations, which he compared with kissing the earth with your feet, and tried to concentrate on slowly setting one foot in front of the other, mindful of the imprints I left behind and how the cool water refreshed my feet and ankles when a wave rolled onto the shore. An hour later, I returned home feeling calmer, but I knew that I had another two challenging weeks ahead with Christmas coming up in a couple of days.

The day before Christmas Eve, I spoke to a German girlfriend and found solace in her words, which offered me to see the situation from a different perspective:

'You know, this experience is actually a gift, the gift of getting to know yourself, learning to love yourself and be more compassionate with yourself.'

Later that day, something inside me made me drive to the city for an escape to the Art Gallery, a space of silence, freedom, and beauty. After an hour in the gallery, I stepped outside and started wandering aimlessly through the streets of Darlinghurst and Surry Hills, not knowing where to go. I felt lonely amidst the many people populating the streets, men and women finishing their last-minute gift shopping and Saturday chores; gay couples passing by hand-in-hand, smiling; a Christmas party group of men in fancy dress staggering out of a restaurant and discussing how to get home. 'Let's call an Uber,' I overheard their conversation and thought: 'You better not drive home yourselves.'

After half an hour of walking down Crown Street, I felt thirsty and stopped at a bar where two women sat at the window looking out to the street. I took a chair next to them and ordered a lemon, lime and bitters. The barman mixed my drink, and I wondered what he thought who I was here. It was 5 pm, apart from the other women no one else was there, and I silently sipped my refreshing drink watching the street and passers-by. I felt like a stranger in this suburb, as if everyone could tell that I didn't belong here; a middle-aged woman, well dressed, wandering the streets alone seeking something, but what?

On my way back, I chose some back streets, which were almost deserted and passed my lawyer's office, which reminded me again of our lovely breakfast meeting. We had already spoken about going out for dinner after my case would have settled.

But before that, I had to manage what would become the saddest and most challenging Christmas Eve I had ever experienced in my life. In the morning of the 24th December, I received an email from my lawyer who had finally read my Christmas card: 'Dear Bettina, I read your card. Thank you. I hope today is as nice as possible. I will sing Stille Nacht for you in Deutsch.'

Tears filled my eyes again when I read his words and I sat on my red sofa for a while, weeping silently. This all-encompassing loneliness followed me wherever I went. I moved around the house in this nothingness, in free fall through this void that had opened up the day before; there was nowhere to cling to, no security net, just this huge emptiness.

It would be the last Christmas in our family home. We played traditional German Christmas carols. In the afternoon, as it is tradition in Germany, we placed the presents for the boys under the tree. Then, we sat down for dinner. Everything looked like it used to be for the past nine years. Like a robot, I had prepared the food, set the table, lit a candle, and we all sat down in silence. I tried hard not to cry over dinner. Suddenly, the music had stopped and the silence was unbearable. I got up and played another CD, this time the fun Australian Christmas songs.

I hardly listened to the conversation between my husband and the boys. I felt estranged, out of place, like I didn't belong to this family, to this Christmas dinner. The meal was much shorter than it used to be and, as it was tradition, the boys got to unwrap their presents afterwards.

After Max had unwrapped his new keyboard and mouse for his computer, he came over to my husband, hugged him and said: 'Thank you, Dad.' Then, he approached me: 'Thank you, Mum,' and gave me a big hug. I couldn't compose myself any longer and started crying, holding on to my teenage son. I got up and escaped to the deck outside, weeping in loneliness. There I stayed for the next hour, alone, sipping a cup of tea and surrendering to my grief.

When it was time to leave for church at 8 pm, I asked Max if he wanted to come with me, as he had mentioned earlier that he would think about it. He said yes, and off we went. I was glad to leave the house. The Christmas service turned out to be wonderful and reminded me very much of the services I used to attend in Germany. The church was beautifully decorated with candles and fairy lights who shone in all their glory. It was just bright enough to read the programme and lyrics of the many carols we sang. I was very pleased that they had included Silent Night, one of my favourite Christmas songs. I sang it for my lawyer that night, in English.

Later on, at home, I sat outside alone in the darkness and eventually sipped my glass of bubbles as I used to every Christmas Eve. The long weekend passed in slow motion. I spent most of the time in my room reading, resting and sleeping as the Chinese herbs seemed to finally have a calming effect on my body. I felt sad, lonely, and miserable. I wept a lot. I felt fragile and vulnerable; the shell around my heart was cracked open.

I was looking forward to the New Year when I would have a week by myself to spend in solitude.

GROUNDLESS

"The spiritual journey involves going beyond hope and fear, stepping into unknown territory, continually moving forward."

Pema Chödrön

****

The end of what was one of the most challenging years in my life had arrived. It was the 31st of December 2017, and one year ago, Jay had changed my life with his memorable Kahuna massage. I couldn't stop reminiscing about this day and how this massage had triggered an avalanche of events resulting in the separation from my husband.

Once I was alone in the house, I let go of any routine and surrendered to my emotions. I took some time to reflect on the past twelve months and to set my goals for 2018. I was again overcome by this all-encompassing nothingness within and around me. I caught myself trying to distract me with mundane tasks such as washing, tidying up, cleaning the house – grateful that the cleaner was on holidays for a week. When I was finished I restlessly wandered through the house and ended up at the pool where I started sweeping the leaves and tidying up the deck area. A refreshing dive in the water didn't release the knot in my stomach or fill the void I sensed.

Tears filled my eyes several times during this day and the following days, and I just let them flow. I wept when I rescued a wasp who frantically tried to escape the water; I wept when I thought of the breakfast with my lawyer the week before; I wept when I thought of Christmas Eve and that it had been the last Christmas in our house; I wept when I read a comment to one of my Instagram posts that 'loneliness is an unaccustomed space to let new people into my life'; I wept at the mere thought of all the special people that the Universe had already sent my way; I wept in the car when the radio station played a love song; I wept at church when a woman who I had never met before prayed for me and my family and wished me luck with all the challenges that still lay ahead.

On New Year's Eve, a friend invited me to come to her place but I decided to stay at home, alone, succumbing to whatever would arise that night. After talking to a few friends on the phone, I made myself something to eat, sat outside on the deck and sipped a glass of bubbles while watching the boats making their way to the Harbour Bridge for the fireworks.

Later, I turned the TV on to watch the 9 pm fireworks, still not sure if I would stay up until midnight. But somehow the evening passed. I watched parts of the Countdown Show on ABC, sometimes with the sound off as I couldn't stand the songs. I distracted myself with Instagram, reading posts from people all over the world and checking who had liked my stories. It alleviated the feeling of loneliness that continued to emerge on a regular basis. At some point, I grabbed my journal and noted that I felt calmer, more relaxed and centred, holding the space I found myself in. From time to time I went outside and stood in the darkness soaking in the party vibes from the neighbours around me. There were celebrations going on in several houses in our street and loud music boomed from different directions ending up in a cacophony which was hard to bear. The time passed, and in the last minutes before midnight I filled another glass of bubbles and danced alone into the New Year to John Paul Young's Love is in the Air broadcasted live from the stage outside the Opera House.

When the fireworks finally started to celebrate the start of the New Year, I cried again at the sight of the beautiful display Sydney had put on again for the millions of spectators in the city and all over the world.

I surrendered to whatever came up and thought that this was how it felt to live when your heart was cracked open, when all the barriers have dissolved, when you live life without a shell. And I made a promise to myself not to let the shell close again. Like so often in those days, the words of Pema Chödrön provided solace: "Impermanence becomes vivid in the present moment; so do compassion and wonder and courage. And so does fear. Anyone who stands on the edge of the unknown, fully in the present without reference point, experiences groundlessness."

On the 8th January, the lawyers would be back in his office to complete the paperwork for our property settlement, and I hoped that we could close this chapter once for all. The sale of our house was scheduled for the end of February. In a couple of months, I would be another step closer to start a new chapter of my life.

IF YOU CAN WALK, YOU CAN DANCE

"If you can talk, you can sing. If you can walk, you can dance."

African Proverb

*****

I got up early on New Year's Day, as I had planned to start the year editing my story. I travelled back in time and saw myself sitting in Kukura House, the main building of the retreat, my fingers dancing frantically over my keyboard to capture my memories while they were still vivid in my mind.

I remembered the words from my life writing teacher: "You are a pilgrim of some sorts, on a journey. There's something powerful in observing the world and finding the words to express it. You are a more powerful human being because you have been on that particular journey."

The more I read, the more I realised how significant this past year had been on my journey towards living my truth.

Again, I enjoyed being by myself and carefree. I gave up any routine. I ate when I was hungry and succumbed to whatever feelings would come up. By now, I was used to crying and didn't suppress my emotions any longer.

In the evening of the 1st January, I made another decision that would change my life. I felt in the mood to watch a movie and looked through our small video collection. My eyes rested on Strictly Ballroom. I remembered that this movie featured John Paul Young's hit Love is in the Air as the closing scene, the song that had carried me into the New Year. While I watched the movie, I heard a voice: Go back to dance school.

I found my old dancing shoes from eight years ago in the corner of the shoe cupboard neatly wrapped in a black cloth bag. I tried them on. Memories of my weekly Salsa socials emerged. And I knew what I was going to do: It was time to have some fun on the dance floor again!

Where to start? I googled dance schools on Sydney's Northern Beaches and found Arthur Murray in Brookvale. The studio was only ten minutes from our home, so I filled out an online form to book my complimentary first lesson. A couple of days later, the phone rang and a friendly voice greeted me:

'Hi, this is Arthur Murray Brookvale. I just saw your message. When would you like to come for your complimentary lesson?'

'I am flexible, when does it suit you?'

'What about tomorrow evening, 6 pm?'

The next day, I drove to Brookvale. When I found the studio in a dilapidated building on Pittwater Rd, which I had passed many times in the past nine years without noticing that there was a dance school in it, I became slightly reluctant. But my excitement overruled any doubts, and I climbed up a flight of stairs and found myself in front of a glass door with the Arthur Murray logo and the word "Reception" on it. I took a deep breath and opened the door.

'Hello, my name is Bettina, I have booked a complimentary lesson,' I addressed the guy who was sitting behind a tiny glass desk with a computer.

'Hi Bettina, I am the studio manager. Welcome to Arthur Murray! Please have a seat, and I'll be with you shortly.'

There was a row of replica Louis Ghost Chairs standing on the right side along the wall. I sat down and unpacked my dance shoes. The studio, a large rectangular room with mirrors along two walls and a row of windows facing the street, was empty. I changed my shoes and waited. A few minutes later, the manager approached me to fill out a form with my address details. He also asked if I had any dance experience and what my dancing goals were. I told him about the dance school in Germany, that I had done many years of Jazz Dance, about the Latin Cardio classes and the Salsa and Bachata socials in Manly.

'Great,' he concluded. 'Let me introduce to your dance teacher then.'

At that moment, the curtain at the back of the room lifted and a young guy appeared. He was dressed in black pants, a black shirt with cufflinks, a burgundy tie and a black vest with a silver chain hanging out from the left front pocket. On top, he wore a black-grey scarf loosely hanging over his shoulders - a flamboyant appearance to say the least.

'Bettina, this is Jason, Jason, this is Bettina. She has done quite a bit of dancing.'

We shook hands, and I wondered if it was strategically a good move to tell my teacher that I had done "quite a bit of dancing". I also was not so sure what to think of this guy who seemed to have emerged from a bygone era. But it was too late to pull out and my curiosity overruled my doubts as I followed Jason to the middle of the dance floor.

'Let's start with Foxtrot,' he opened the lesson. He must have seen the slight panic on my face when I mentioned that I hadn't danced Foxtrot since I was 15.

He took my right hand and showed me the basic steps standing next to me. 'It's just walking,' he explained. 'If you can walk, you can dance Foxtrot.'

The minute he turned the music on, offered me his hand and lead me across the floor, all my panic was gone. It felt so good to dance again with a good leader! I succumbed to his strong arms and followed the movement of his body. How much fun I had!

The 45 minutes passed in a flash, and in my first lesson, I had danced Foxtrot, Waltz, Tango, Rumba, Salsa, and Swing. That night, I signed up on the spot for eight private and eight group lessons starting the following week.

My intuition told me that Jason was another one of those new people that the Universe kept sending my way. When I left the studio that evening, I felt happy and in tune with my body and couldn't wait for my next lesson.

GO WHERE YOU FEEL ALIVE

"Dancing is just discovery, discovery, discovery."

Martha Graham

*****

Australia Day 2018. I spent the day at home; tidying up, cleaning and putting the final decorating touches in each of the rooms before the real estate photographer would come the following morning. Everything went to plan. While we prepared the house for sale, the lawyers finalised our property settlement documents. 'We are on the home stretch,' my lawyer reminded me with an encouraging voice that the legal part of the separation would soon be done.

Since I had started dancing again, I felt so much more alive. My dance lessons were the highlight of my days. It was addictive; the more I danced, the more I wanted it. My instructor turned out to be one of my new tribe of people. He was not only an excellent teacher, he proofed to be a wonderful conversation partner. He was a creative soul, a fiction writer, loved reading and drawing. We often talked about yoga, meditation and spirituality. He asked me about my sons and how I got along with them. He even gave me tips how to connect with them during the challenging teenage years. 'I've been there ten years ago,' he added with a cheeky grin on his face.

"Go where you feel the most alive" I read almost daily on the blackboard in the yoga studio. It was the dance school where I felt most alive. Dancing energised my body and nourished my soul.

The first three weeks of the new year passed in a flash. I spent most evenings in the dance school. I booked three private lessons per week plus and joined several group classes. I was welcomed by a new community of people and started to get to know them a bit better each week. After the first couple of weeks, I felt like I was part of the studio for months. Three weeks into my newly found dance life I passed my first dance check with bravura and was upgraded to the Bronze 1 level. I booked another package for four months, which would keep me going until the end of May if I progressed with the same speed. I had not only rekindled my love for dancing, I had also found a new community of people who shared the same passion.

Once a month, the studio offered a social dancing event on a Friday night with a playlist of ballroom and latin music to give students the opportunity to practise. Enthusiastic about all the new dance moves I had just learned, I couldn't wait to get to my first Friday night social. As I didn't know a lot of people yet, one woman started a conversation:

'Are you coming to the Leichhardt showcase in April?' she wanted to know.

'Leichhardt showcase, what's that?'

'Oh, they do that every year. It's basically a day where the students perform their dances in front of an audience, all dressed up like the professionals. You can participate or just go and watch. In the evening, there's a ball,' she explained.

I was hooked. That sounded interesting, and I wanted to find out more about it. The following weekend, I googled the event and came across a selection of images showing the dance teachers of our studio on the floor with some of the students I had already met. They looked stunning in beautiful ballroom and sexy latin dresses. At that moment, I made the decision to dance at the Leichhardt showcase in April.

'What do I have to do to dance with you at the Leichhardt showcase?' I asked my teacher in my next lesson.

'Well, we have to talk to the studio manager first and then work out what you want to do,' he replied as if I had just asked him to meet me for a coffee somewhere.

'Oh my God, I am so excited! I always wanted to wear some of those dresses,' I kept daydreaming.

'That can be arranged,' Jason replied with a wink. 'We have a selection of dresses in our store room. Some are for sale, others can be hired.'

'Really?' I couldn't believe that my dream was actually not so far out of reach as I had assumed.

The week after, I found myself in the store room trying on ballroom dresses. Some of the dresses were so stunning that I was lost for words. A couple of them seemed to have waited for me. They fitted perfectly. I felt comfortable wearing them and visualised myself dancing in them at the showcase.

'What do you think of this one?' one of the female instructors pulled out a black, backless number with a high neck and embellished with pink and orange lace flower applications in a diagonal pattern on the front. The skirt covered the knee on the right side but was draped up on the left to uncover the leg. But what I loved most about it was the pink and orange ostrich feather edging of the skirt. I had always adored feathers and having them bouncing around my legs while dancing Rumba, Cha-Cha, and Salsa was just spectacular. Similar to the first dress, it seemed to be custom-made for me.

That evening, on my way home, I was in a state of excitement and couldn't wait to show the world the pictures of me wearing these dresses. Now I was even more determined to learn and improve my dances as quickly as possible. The 7th of April was only ten weeks away.

SOLD

"Surrender – what an amazingly powerful word. It often engenders the thought of weakness and cowardice. In my case, it required all the strength I had to be brave enough to follow the invisible into the unknown."

Michael A. Singer, The Surrender Experiment

*****

On the first weekend in February, our family home went on the market for sale. The month was jam-packed with the twice weekly open houses, the final appointments with my lawyer to sign the property settlement, the initial meeting with my new financial advisor, house hunting for a new place to live, work commitments, and dance lessons almost every evening. My habit of colour-coding my daily tasks in my diary turned out to be very helpful, and the days didn't seem to have enough hours for what I wanted to get done.

 I would get up at 5 am to either start the day with a 6 am yoga class or a writing session. Once my husband and the boys were out of the house, I started working until it was time to pick up Valentin from the bus stop around 4 pm. Then, I would finish my work, prepare something for dinner and disappear to the dance school for either a private class or a group lesson. I often tried to combine the two to make most out of my time in the studio. In the lead up to the Leichhardt showcase, I ended up having three to four private classes a week. By the time I returned home, had something to eat and a shower, it was often 10 pm, and I would fall into my bed, tired and happy.

After talking to my teacher, I decided to dance Waltz, Tango, Argentine Tango, Swing, Cha-Cha, Rumba, Salsa, Mambo, Bachata, the Peabody and the Lindy Hop at the showcase.

Dancing had become a vital part of my days and weeks, and I wondered how I had survived without it for so many years. In preparation for the event, I decided to purchase the black Latin dress that I had tried on. It cost my a small fortune but it came with lots of fun and balm for my soul. My time at the studio turned out to be so much more than just dancing, it was an act of self-love, of connecting with like-minded people, of celebrating all that I had achieved so far. The studio had become my happy place.

Mid-February, the lawyers lodged our papers to the court. Now, it was a waiting game.

At the end of the month, my husband and I pondered about pushing back the auction for another couple of weeks because there was only one seriously interested party. Every day, I prayed to the Universe to send us enough buyers to make the auction a success. Two days before the auction, our agent informed us that another interested buyer had turned up and that we would have two parties bidding.

On the 28th of February, at 5 pm, I entered the auction rooms in Mosman with anticipation and the familiar tightness in my stomach. The room was already filled with groups of people, some sitting, some standing. Several agents kept pacing around the floor to greet their vendors and buyers and to make sure that everyone who wanted to bid was registered. Everyone was talking in low voices, some whispered, heads together, not to let anyone in their conversation or give anything away. Gazes were exchanged, wandering from the conversation partner to the large electronic billboard which listed the upcoming auctions. Our house was the last one.

Images from our decks and pool with sweeping harbour views appeared only to fade away after a few seconds. There was no doubt that we would sell our beautiful home of ten years that night. With a cup of green tea, I was standing by myself in the waiting area outside the auction rooms, and emotions creeped up in my body. From time to time I was interrupted in my thoughts from someone who passed by and asked if I was ok and if I didn't want to take a seat inside. I was not so sure if I wanted to sit inside or rather watch from the distance. I observed the other people around me and tried to spot other vendors who, like me, seemed to be slightly nervous and kept moving around restlessly. I waited for my husband who was on his way from the airport and hoped that he would make it on time.

Then, the auction started. The first property was passed in, as there was only one bidder. After a few minutes, I decided to take a seat in the back of the auction room. I listened and watched. One property after the other came up for sale, and I felt for the other vendors when the hammer fell. I messaged my lawyer for mental support. He replied instantly, wished me luck and asked me to let him know the outcome. The auctioneer had just called up the second last property and started his usual spiel. Finally, our house appeared on the big screen. I took three deep breaths and asked the Universe for a successful sale. One of the registered bidders started the process with his first bid. The auctioneer repeated the bid which appeared instantly on the screen. He kept talking and asking for more. Silence. I looked around to spot the other buyer but couldn't see him.

'Where is this other couple you showed me before?' I whispered in my husband's direction.

'I don't know, I can't see them either.'

The auctioneer kept praising the proportions of our home and how magnificent it was. He repeated his question for higher bids.

'They can't sell the house for this price, can they? And, where is Cameron?' I addressed my husband with a slight panic in my voice and wondered where our agent had disappeared.

'No, it's way under our reserve.'

Suddenly, I saw our agent rushing into the room followed by the bidder, who entered the room bare foot, carrying his shoes in one hand rushing towards the front of the room seemingly out of breath. I couldn't believe my eyes. As soon as he sat down, he topped the previous bid.

'Now, we are in the game,' I heard the auctioneer.

The bidding continued until the first bidder was out. As we still had not reached our reserve price, Cameron asked us in a small meeting room to start the negotiations. We decided to push the buyer further knowing about the risk of losing him. My nerves were on edge. After a while, Cameron came back and said that he couldn't push the buyer any further or we would run the risk of not selling the property. We decided to agree, went outside to confirm with the auctioneer, and the hammer fell.

'Sold!' The noise of the hammer was loud and hit me right in the stomach.

The audience clapped their hands, the buyer got up from his seat, with his shoes on, and came towards us.

'Congratulations!'

Cameron congratulated us on the sale of our house. Everyone smiled in excitement. I shook hands and smiled back with emotions coming up. Was I going to cry in front of everyone? Wasn't this the start of the new chapter of my life I was looking forward to? Or, as my lawyer had put it in his text message before, the end of all the lengthy negotiations over the past eight months?

I managed to stay calm, smiling at the new owner of our home when I shook his hand. 'Bless it with love and let it go,' words from a friend came into my mind.

'I hope you'll enjoy it,' I even heard myself saying.

'We will.'

Not long after, we left the agent's offices. I wandered down the street by myself. Very slowly, as I still had to come to terms with the fact that we had just sold our home of ten years. A big milestone on my journey which had started nine months before. In six weeks I would need to move out. I still had no idea where I would live. I felt homeless. Images from ten years ago emerged. I saw myself standing in front of our house in Wiesbaden when the big container with all our belongings was closed to start its long journey to Australia. While I walked to my car, I knew that I could trust the Universe that a place for my sons and me would turn up on time.

MY NEW HOME

"There are short-cuts to happiness, and dancing is one of them."

Vicky Baum, Writer and Author

*****

The following weekend, I sat down with the checklist from our agent to prepare the settlement, which was the standard 42 days. I would need to move out by mid-April which meant that I needed to reinforce my house hunting activities. There were quite a few 3-bedroom properties on the market but I still hadn't found the right one.

Inspired by one of Louise Hay's books, I had been repeating positive affirmations for months; that I would find a wonderful place, preferably a townhouse or duplex, that suited my needs. I was looking for something low-maintenance that I could transform into a personal home which would reflect my love for art and beautiful things. The boys would have decent sized bedrooms where they would feel at home when they stayed with me.

On the Saturday after the auction, I was out and about to inspect several properties but none of the places spoke to me. As I had learned that I could rely on my intuition, I usually decided within the first minute in a property if 'it felt right' or if it didn't. I trusted my gut.

The morning passed, nothing had taken my fancy, and I sat down in a little coffeeshop to bridge 30 minutes before the next inspection. I even contemplated of returning home, as the property was located in a street where I had inspected another place a few weeks earlier and turned it down because of the noise levels coming from the nearby three-lane main road.

But something made me go. The two-level brick townhouse was set back from the street and one of two strata titles on the property. The moment I entered I was pleasantly surprised. After passing the small entrance area, I walked in an open rectangular living space with a U-shaped kitchen on one side and a separate open area, which was set up as dining room, on the other. I loved the fact that although it was all open plan, it had distinct areas to decorate. There was also a laundry, internal access to the adjacent garage, and a small courtyard wrapping around the house. Upstairs, I found two bright bedrooms, the main bathroom, the master bedroom with ensuite and a small balcony overlooking the district.

The longer I wandered through the house, the more I felt at ease with it. There was some renovation work to do but overall this property ticked most of my boxes and I could see myself living there.

On my way home in the car, I felt in good spirits, as this was a place I wanted to research further. I emailed the web link to our agent, who had offered his help to find a home and to navigate the auction process if needed. In the next days, I agreed with him on a strategy how to best move forward. He also gave me an indication of the price I should expect to pay.

The following Wednesday, I returned to make sure that I still had the same feelings about the place. I stayed for the entire 30 minutes, worked out how and where I would place my furniture and just soaked in the atmosphere and how it would feel to live in this house. My gut told me the same story as three days before. I discussed the next steps with the sales agent, told her that I was happy to bid at the auction and that she should alert me if someone else put an offer in before the auction.

The same afternoon, Cameron called to let us know that the buyers of our house had asked for an extended settlement. After a short discussion, we offered them 60 instead of 42 days, which would postpone my move until the first week of May. This was perfect timing, as the property I was looking at had a 42-day settlement as well, which would allow me to move straight from our house into the new place. I thanked the Universe.

The following week, the sales agent informed us that she had got an offer for the townhouse from another party. I informed Cameron who started the bidding via text messages. On the Thursday afternoon, while I was at a dance lesson, I instructed him to increase our bid in the hope that the other party would drop out. The waiting game was nerve-wracking. A few hours later, I still hadn't heard anything back. It was 7 pm by now, and I was mentally exhausted. At 8 pm, I finally got a message that there had been no higher bid placed and that the owner of the property would make a decision the next morning.

I fell into a deep sleep. The next morning, 23rd March 2018, positive news was waiting for me when I picked up my phone. "Congratulations, they accepted your offer! Exchange of contracts tomorrow," I read on my text thread. A heavy weight lifted from my shoulders. It was Friday and I was looking forward to an evening at the dance school where I would celebrate my victory with a glass of champagne with my new friends. I had passed another milestone and would move into my new home at the end of April.

And there were more exciting news coming. After a long day of emails and phone calls with the agent and conveyancer, I received a text message from my lawyer: "Hello warrior queen, just checked the court's computer system, your order was made. Open the champagne!"

My heart wanted to jump out of my chest. After fifteen months of living in uncertainty and six weeks of waiting for the court's final decision, a wave of relief and liberation washed over me. I had found a new home and the court had signed our settlement papers. In good spirit and with a bottle of champagne in my bag, I jumped in my car and drove to the dance school to celebrate the purchase of my new home at our monthly social dancing night.

At these events, we danced smooth and rhythm dances to a random playlist. I was especially looking forward to the Argentine Tango, one of the most sophisticated and classy dances that I had only recently discovered and started learning. When the Argentine Tango came up, Jason approached me, looked me in the eyes and, without a word, put his arm around me. He started to walk, leading me softly across the floor. I succumbed to his moves, following blindly. The longer we danced, the less I could remember what I was doing. I didn't know if anyone else was dancing as we were crossing the dance floor, moving forward, backwards, turning. Everything around me seemed to disappear, to retreat; My mind shut out all the voices, the chatter, the laughing of the other dancers. I was alone with my dance partner, feeling his warm body pressed against mine and hearing his breathing very close to my ear. He drowned out the crowd. There was energy flowing through our bodies. It was a conversation without words. Unfortunately, the music stopped suddenly and I was thrown back into reality. 'Beautiful,' I heard him say while he let go of our embrace position. It took a few seconds to find myself again in the room with all the other dancers. I still didn't know if anybody else had joined us or if they had watched us dance. All I knew was that I wanted more of what I had just experienced.

The following Monday, my husband moved out. The removalists arrived early and had loaded his furniture and boxes by 10 am. I was sitting in front of my computer in the study when I heard his voice behind me:

'I'm leaving now,' he said as if he was going to work. 'I'll call later, and we can talk about the next weekend.'

'Ok,' I replied.

A few seconds later, I heard the front door close. I was alone. Everything I had wished for in the past ten months had finally happened. I was unsure of how I would cope with my new normal.

This would be my first week alone in our large, and by now half empty house, as the boys would stay with my husband the next seven days according to our parenting plan. When I had dropped them off at the bus stop in the morning, I was on the brink of tears knowing that they would not return home in the afternoon. Valentin also had to find his new school bus including changing buses on his way home. In the afternoon, when it was time to pick him up at the bus stop, I dialled his mobile number.

'Hi, it's Mum. Where are you? Did you find the new buses?

'Yes, I'm already home,' he replied calmly. 'No problem with the buses, and there's a boy from Year 9 who is taking the same bus. He's living up the road.'

I realised how grown up my 13-year-old was and that I didn't need to worry about him adjusting to the new situation.

In the evening, I stayed at the dance school longer the usual. Being in the half empty house for only a few hours had created a void which was hard to cope with. I didn't want to be alone at home that night. Dancing and mingling with my friends was a welcome distraction. When I left the school, I expressed my feelings to my teacher.

'It's great to be alone in a big house!' he exclaimed. 'Get a pizza, a glass of red wine, and light a candle.'

As I was hungry anyway, I followed his advice and found myself enjoying my dinner and newly found freedom in our abandoned family home. While I was eating, I looked around the empty living room with only one standing light and a small side table left. Suddenly, I saw the opportunity to use this space as the perfect dance floor to practise for the upcoming showcase.

*****

Six weeks later, at the end of April 2018, I moved into my new home. Downsizing to a much smaller home took a bit of adjustment, but I knew I had done it years ago in Germany. So I found myself 'walking the talk' following the 5-step process to downsizing with style that I had laid out in my self-published book of the same title.

To make the space my own, I had all the carpet and laminate floor removed before I moved in and had a beautiful new timber floor laid throughout the house. I chose a white-washed European Oak to brighten up the entire place. Over the next twelve months, I renovated the small upstairs balcony, the downstairs courtyard and installed a beautifully designed and powder-coated metal gate featuring cut-out gingko leaves. Inside, I mixed and matched the few smaller furniture pieces, which I taken from our family home. I was never fond of having everything in the same style or purchasing entire room fit outs from a store. In all the places I lived, I always followed the advice that I had given the readers of my book, namely to only choose furniture pieces that spoke to them in some way, pieces that made them happy.

I also bought a few missing items: New beds for my sons and a dining table for the living room downstairs. I started looking around for new and second hand tables and couldn't make up my mind. One day, at an Arbonne meeting with our team, one of my business partners who had just moved into a new house, asked if someone needed a dining table, as she wanted to sell one of hers. The table fitted size-wise and had an interesting top from recycled timber. I took it as another sign from the Universe and bought it.

My beloved bookshelf, the only large item I had taken from our family home, fitted perfectly on the wall in the rectangular room next to the main living area. I decorated a cosy reading corner and set up my home office on the opposite side of the room.

Thanks to my interior design and room planning knowledge, I had measured and drawn up the floor plan beforehand and planned the layout of every room including my furniture pieces. On the day of the move, Max and I knew exactly where every single piece had to go and directed the removalists accordingly. As the garage was too small for my car and got a lot of natural light through a north-facing window, I transformed it into a storage and art room. Although I had de-cluttered lots of my art stuff, I couldn't throw out everything and had a few boxes of art supplies and several canvasses that I stored on a suspended storage rack under the garage ceiling. Our old dining table ended up as work space.

I also had plans to renovate the kitchen, laundry, and ensuite, which were functioning but in original condition from when the house was built in the 1980s. So I decided to live in the house for a while to figure out with which room to start. However, I was not aware how my dancing journey would unfold. When the time came to book my dancing trips in 2019, I had to make a few monetary decisions: renovations or dance trips? I didn't have to think very long about that, and the renovations were postponed.

LET'S DANCE

"Dance is the hidden language of the soul."

Martha Graham

*****

The day started early. I got up at 5 am and applied a thick layer of makeup appropriate for my first dance showcase on the 7th April 2018. At 6 am, my hair stylist arrived. To match my beautiful dress, I had bought some hair accessories in rose gold, which she skilfully worked into my hair to create a work of art on my head. A couple of days before, I had my body spray-tanned for the first time in my life, something I thought I would never do.

After she had left, I grabbed my dresses and bag and went again through my checklist with everything I thought I would need for a 15-hour dance event. At 7 am, I left the house to drive to Sydney's Inner West.

When I arrived at the Albert Palais in Leichhardt, I could sense the excitement in the air. The ladies' change room was buzzing with dancers trying to find a space for their belongings and dresses. I placed my bag in a corner, found an empty space on one of the coat hangers and went upstairs to familiarise myself with the location. The Grand Ballroom was a large rectangular space with magnificent chandeliers above a beautiful dance floor surrounded by round tables, which were allocated to the different Arthur Murray studios across Sydney. On the far side of the room, along the wall, the four judges had their seats on an elevated stage. What I liked about this event was the fact that I would get feedback to my dancing from four professionals looking at my posture, foot work, and styling.

I found a seat at a table where a fellow dancer from our studio had already made himself comfortable. I said a quick hello and returned to the change room downstairs to get ready for the smooth dances. For Waltz and Tango, I had chosen a simple but elegant black dress from my wardrobe and simply added my sparkling, shiny rose gold bracelets, ring, and ear rings matching the hair accessories.

'You look lovely,' Jason greeted me with a smile when he first saw me.

I sat down at our table while the room filled quickly. The first heats started at 8 am with the Country/Western and New Vogue dances. I watched my fellow students and the other competitors while I was waiting for my first gig on the dance floor. My hands felt like ice blocks and I tried to concentrate on slow breathing and silently repeated positive affirmations that everything would be fine. Was I really here? Dancing at a showcase with my wonderful teacher?

I looked at my list of my entries: Waltz, Tango, Cha-Cha, Rumba, Swing, Mambo, Salsa, Bachata, the Peabody, the Lindy Hop, and the Argentine Tango. It all felt so unreal. The day promised to be exciting with the showcase dancing until late afternoon followed by a dinner, dance performances and a party until late.

More students from our studio arrived and pulled me out of my daydream back to reality. My first heat was at 9 am and I waited with cold hands and the usual tightness in my stomach when I was nervous. I took more deep breaths.

When it was my turn, I followed Jason to the floor. My initial nervousness turned into excitement after the first Waltz and Tango. After the smooth dances in the morning, the afternoon was dedicated to the rhythm and speciality dances, one of which was the Argentine Tango.

I silently prayed to the Universe not to stuff this up. My heart was beating so loudly that I thought every single person in the audience could hear it. Jason offered me his right hand, and I took it willingly. My palms were cold and I tried to tune out the people around me. I still had to pinch myself that a dream was

about to come true: I was wearing one of these stunning latin dresses that I had admired so often in TV shows and was about to dance my favourite dance.

Everything seemed so unreal. The judges were waiting for the couples to take their positions on the dance floor. I didn't want to ruin the next one and a half minutes for which I had practised over the past eight weeks. I slowly set one foot in front of the other walking side-by-side with my teacher to the middle of the floor.

From the day we first met Jason had caught my attention because of his distinct style and non-conformist approach to every-day life. We had had many thought-provoking conversations during my dance classes, and I treasured his opinion on things that occupied my mind in times of change. He never failed to surprise me with his answers, and I followed his suggestions more than once only to discover a new perspective on things that mattered to me. I had to admit that my dance teacher had become a special person in my life. I had only known him for three months, but I could feel a soul connection to this man who could be my son.

We walked onto the dance floor. The feather decorated skirt of my sparkling black Latin dress with intricate pink and orange flower applications swung elegantly around my legs. My black dance shoes were embellished with silver beaded buckles. Jason turned around and pulled me into close Tango embrace.

'Let's dance, shall we?'

CIAO AMORE PRAGUE

"In the middle of every difficulty lies opportunity."

Albert Einstein

*****

Unfortunately, the showcase in Leichhardt was the last event I danced with Jason. He suffered an injury and had to stop dancing for months. In September 2018, after three months of dancing with almost every other teacher in the studio, I sought a conversation with the studio owner to discuss how to move forward. Fortunately, she opened the conversation that she had just found a new senior instructor, Italian and ex-Latin Professional.

'His name is Daniele, he is very experienced and tall,' she tried to convince me beforehand.

I agreed to have a trial practice to see whether I was happy to continue dancing with him.

When he arrived to our first lesson, he greeted me with a big smile:

'Ciao, I'm Daniele, nice to meet you,' he introduced himself with his charming Italian accent and a firm handshake.

I returned the smile: 'Hi, I'm Bettina, nice to meet you too.'

I was relieved, he was tall enough and seemed to be a nice guy.

We started dancing foxtrot. As I had just advanced to Bronze 3, it felt like a completely new dance. The steps and timing were very different to what I had learned previously. It didn't take long and we were laughing and chatting as if we had known each other for a long time. I was happy and grateful, as I knew I had found another member of my soul family.

'I am here to check you out, because I am looking for a new teacher' I joked with a cheeky grin on my face. He laughed and we kept dancing. He turned out to be an outstanding instructor and a wonderful person to hang out with. I believe our common European background contributed to our instant connection, as Daniele described it a few weeks later.

Over time, I learned a bit more about his family in Italy, his professional dancing career and that he only wanted to stay for a few months in Australia when he visited the first time. Then, in 2012, he took a leap of faith and moved Down Under. He soon started teaching at one of the other Arthur Murray studios in Sydney before he moved on to the City studio where we met.

Dancing my first international ProAm Ballroom competition in Prague, the All Round Championship, was the highlight of my dancing year 2019. Around Christmas the year before, one of the instructors had asked me casually if I was planning to go to Prague. The organisers had just announced the venue for the European Arthur Murray Dance-o-Rama (DOR) CIAO Amore. I was about to finish my first year at the dance school, and I had never been to any dance competition before.

I was slightly intimidated by the thought of dancing and competing with people from all over the world when I asked Daniele what he thought of it. He assured me that I would be doing fine. Although we only had been dancing together for three months, I trusted his professional advice and ability to assess my potential and started planning this once-in-a-lifetime trip to the Czech Republic in July 2019.

Over the Christmas holidays, I reflected on my dancing goals for the coming year and decided to focus on improving my Smooth dances. I also noted that I would participate in two Arthur Murray showcases in Sydney in April and November, one in

Adelaide in June, and the international event in Prague in August. I had eight months to prepare for it. And as I had never been in the capital of the Czech Republic before, I planned to combine this trip with a holiday in Germany afterwards. I liked the idea of combining dancing and traveling as long as I was fit and healthy to do it.

When the dance school reopened in January 2019, I told Daniele about my ambitious goals. I asked him to point out everything I needed to improve in Waltz, foxtrot, and Tango and to push me out of my comfort zone. As the weeks went by, I started noticing significant improvements in those dances and even started to learn a new dance: The Viennese Waltz.

Because of my goals and schedule, I increased my private lessons from four to six lessons a week, plus attended one or two group classes in the lead up to the events. Some weeks, I found myself in the dance school every night except the weekends, when they were closed, and which I needed to rest my body and feet.

Time seemed to fly and suddenly Prague was only four weeks away. I squeezed in as many private lessons as possible and usually went three to four days a week to the dance school. As I had asked him, Daniele often pushed me to my limits with layers and layers of technique to put into practice. "You asked me to do so and you have so much potential in ballroom because of your height and long legs. So use them," he would often repeat when I whinged about his never-ending demands.

Sometimes, I was mentally and physically so exhausted that I couldn't concentrate anymore, and all I felt was lower back pain and the desire to put my feet up. A relaxing bath with Epsom salts would do wonders.

The day of my departure came, and together with two other students, we made our way to Europe. Connected via a Facebook Messenger group, we kept each other informed on the stages of our journeys, as we were all in different planes and had different arrival times in Prague.

The plan was to meet up in the Hilton Hotel, the venue for the DOR, and where we all stayed for the week. A friend of mine and I had decided to arrive on the Sunday, two days before the official start of the event. After I had made my way to the hotel, I checked in and unpacked my luggage. I had carried my precious ballroom gowns, my shoes and accessories as hand luggage after an experienced dancer had advised me not to check in the dresses and shoes in case they would not arrive in Prague.

'Are you sure that's necessary?' I had asked in disbelief and not really wanting to carry the heavy ballroom gowns with me on a 28-hour trip where I had to change planes twice, first in Dubai, then in Frankfurt.

'You decide what you want to do, but I can tell you I met dancers who had nothing to wear the day before the competition. And you definitely don't want to have to compete in a dress you have never worn before and new shoes,' she went on.

After considering the pros and cons of checking in the dresses or carrying them through three airports, I decided to pack them in a separate clothes hanger bag, which I could take into the plane. As I was flying business class, the extra hand luggage was not be an issue.

When I finally unpacked and hung up my four ballroom gowns, I was happy to see that they hadn't suffered any damage during the long trip and sent a gratitude prayer to the dancer who had convinced me to take them as hand luggage.

Not long after, I met my friend in the lobby and we headed to the Hilton rooftop bar with stunning views over Prague's Old Town to celebrate the start our week of dancing with a glass of bubbles.

Over the next couple of days, more and more students, teachers, and judges arrived at the hotel, which seemed to be invaded by dancers. From the lobby, to the restaurant, the lifts, and the corridors, you could hear excited voices in different languages chattering about the upcoming competition.

On Monday and Tuesday, I explored the city by bus, boat and foot and sorted out the schedule with the hairstylist I had booked online. As I didn't trust the Russian mob who were the official hair and makeup stylists, I had organised my own stylist from a local hairdressing salon via the Internet. As the other two students from our studio wanted to use her as well, the salon agreed that she would come to the hotel each morning at 5:30am to do our hair.

The day before the dancing started, I ran into a woman in the lobby with a desperate look on her face. I can't recall how our conversation started but I do remember that she told me that her entire luggage got lost at Amsterdam airport where she had to change planes coming from the US and that she had no spare clothes besides the ones she was wearing and that she was missing all her competition dresses and shoes. I sent another prayer of gratitude to the lady who urged me to carry my dresses by hand.

On Tuesday night, the event kicked off with a welcome dinner at the hotel. The organisers, an Italian couple who ran the majority of the Arthur Murray studios in Italy, informed us that there were over 400 participants and spectators from Australia, Canada, USA, Lebanon, Poland, Romania, Ukraine, UK, UAE, and Italy. As a result, with over 16,500 entries in over 400 heats, the event would kick-off on Wednesday night already with the solo routines, the Speciality Smooth dances (Argentine Tango, Milonga, Tango Vals) and the Speciality Rhythm dances (Salsa, Bachata, Merengue). As I had entries in all these categories, I had to be in the ballroom at 6pm.

In the afternoon, I found myself exhausted and tired from half a day of sightseeing in the soaring summer heat of Prague followed by a three-hour hairdresser session to colour, wash, blow-dry, and style my hair. I nearly fell asleep in the salon.

When I entered the ballroom that evening, I felt so tired that I thought I would not be able to make my first night of dancing.

'Have some of your Fizz Sticks,' Daniele looked at me with a cheeky grin on his face and pointing to the pile of energy drink sachets in front of me.

First up, the solo routine. We were entry number 51 from 88 solo performances in total. The closer our turn came, the more nervous I became. When the couple with number 49 was on the floor, Daniele looked at me and nodded his head: 'Let's go. Relax and just have fun. You know your steps.' Yes, we had danced this one-minute-thirty-seconds piece over and over again, and still, I was shaking inside.

'Solo routine, number 51, Argentine Tango, Bettina and Daniele from the Sydney studio,' the organiser introduced us to the crowd. Daniele took my left hand and guided me in the middle of the dance floor which looked gigantic in that moment. My heart pounded in my chest, and I took a few deep breaths to concentrate on the first steps. The music started and Daniele walked towards me turning me in front of him into a shadow position. We danced one of my favourite dances and I again felt the deep connection to my teacher, whom I had been dancing with for almost a year. It all went well, including the lift, and one minute thirty passed in a flash. The people applauded, Daniele pressed a kiss to my cheek, and we disappeared from the spotlight into the anonymous mass of spectators.

Several energy drinks later, and after the long session of solo routines was finished, I was dancing again in the Closed Smooth and Rhythm Speciality events. Despite the fact that my body wanted to rest and sleep, the adrenalin kept me going until the very end.

It was after 11pm when I finally found myself in my hotel room, happy and exhausted, only to spend another half an hour to get rid of my makeup and clips that were entangled in my hair which seemed to be glued to my head. After a shower, I fell into my bed still on an adrenaline high which made it hard to fall asleep despite the all-encompassing exhaustion.

I can't remember how long I slept. When the alarm clock brutally ripped me out of my sleep at 5am for our 5:30am appointment with the hairstylist, I felt like I had just laid down and dragged myself into the bathroom to put on my makeup half asleep. This procedure repeated every morning for four days during which I was not allowed to wash my hair. Welcome to the world of ballroom dancing!

After the first day, we all got used to living in this bubble of glitz and glamour constantly wearing thick layers of makeup and hair spray. We hardly left the hotel, as our schedule kept us moving between our rooms where we changed dresses and the Grand Ballroom where the dancing happened. Sometimes, I had a longer break between heats, which allowed a welcome rest on my bed. Any opportunity to put my feet up was welcomed. However, always mindful of not destroying the hair styling, which meant that I was more sitting in my bed than actually lying down.

On day two, I was looking forward to one of the highlights of the whole week: the All Round Championship. This was a knockout competition in Smooth and Rhythm dances. Only after the couples were called on the floor, the organiser revealed the dances. In my first rounds, I started with Tango and Foxtrot as Smooth dances and with ChaCha and Rumba in the Rhythm heat. After all couples had danced the first round, we were called back to the semi-finals and to the finals, where I had to dance the Foxtrot and another Rumba with five other couples. I ended up on place six and was super happy to have made it that far among all the international dancers.

Our evening outings were pretty spectacular and something I won't forget. On Friday night, we had to dress up in costumes from a bygone era, and our studio chose the Roaring Twenties. We didn't know where we would go and were told to meet in the lobby at 7pm. The lower lobby filled with at least 250 people in a kaleidoscope of colours and fancy costumes chatting and laughing in curious excitement about the evening to unfold.

Suddenly, a row of red, black, and beige vintage cars arrived at the hotel entrance to pick us up - one group after the other – and drive us along the cobblestones of Prague to the magnificent Žofín Palace, a Neo-Renaissance building on an island in the Vitava river. We felt like royals waving at the strolling tourists with long cigarette holders in our hands. When we arrived at the venue, finger food and champagne awaited us. We gathered on the lawn in front of the palace until the last group had arrived.

An impressive staircase led us to the first floor and into the ballroom. What caught my eye instantly was the ceiling with the most stunning paintings, decorative elements, and chandeliers. A light show illuminated the room with changing colours spotlighting the architectural elements and bathing the space in a magic atmosphere. Shivers ran over my body and I had to pinch myself that I was lucky to be part of this unforgettable evening. Big round tables beautifully decorated framed the dance floor. Not long, and the floor was packed with couples enjoying more dancing after the competition during the day.

Again, it was almost midnight until we returned to the hotel knowing that the alarm clock would ring mercilessly in a few hours.

On the last day of the competition, all amateur dancers finished early afternoon. As much as I had enjoyed this week of dancing, I felt relieved and couldn't wait to get into the shower to wash my hair. It needed several loads of shampoo and conditioner to get rid of all the hairspray that had accumulated on my head over four days.

I indulged in a nap before I got ready for the final ball on Saturday night. It was black tie and long dresses, and I loved how the ballroom changed into an elegant setting for our final gathering. During dinner, the professionals performed in their competition, which was the highlight of the evening. I recorded several couples particularly to watch and copy the ladies' arm styling. Again, I felt so grateful and happy to spend time among my dancer friends who all shared the same passion and seemed to be connected with invisible threads.

At the very end of the evening, each studio from around the world was called on the floor, and we created a big circle of Arthur Murray dancers holding hands to Michael Jackson's song 'Heal the World'. There were a lot of teary eyes shimmering in the dimmed light, and I am sure that none of us wanted this event to be over. Then, the organiser asked each person to turn around, say *Hi* and have a dance with someone they hadn't danced with during the week. I found myself facing an Italian guy and had a nice chat while dancing Nightclub Two Step.

The next morning, our studio met for breakfast the last time and a sense of nostalgia lingered in the air. Was it really all over already? Sadness spread all over my body. None of us wanted that last breakfast to end, however, checkout was at 10 am and we had to return to our rooms to get ready.

Afterwards, I met with my friends in the lobby a last time before we headed to the airport. Daniele appeared and said farewell hugging all of us. Then he disappeared with his suitcase outside the hotel. My heart felt heavy because I knew I would not see him for nine weeks, as he went on a prolonged holiday in Europe with his girlfriend.

Not long after, one of my friends and I shared a taxi to the airport. Our planes to Frankfurt and Zurich left from the same terminal and we spent a couple of hours together waiting for our departure. Sitting in the plane, I watched my dancing videos non-stop for an hour reminiscing the wonderful week in Prague until we touched down in Germany. I wanted to fill my mind with the beautiful memories before I would face what was waiting for me in my home town.

THE FUNERAL

"A man must not be afraid of death; however, he must fear never starting to live."

Marcus Aurelius

*****

Five days before I was boarding my plane to Prague via Abu Dhabi and Frankfurt, I answered a phone call from my aunt in Germany.

'Hey Rosa, how are you?' I tried to sound as normal as possible suppressing the dark forebodings that a call on a Monday afternoon, 4 pm, had triggered when I saw my aunt's name on the display. She was the wife of my mother's youngest brother and my go-to person in Germany after we had moved to Australia. We usually only called each other on the weekends after arranging a time via WhatsApp.

'I am afraid, I have bad news Bettina,' I heard her say with a worried tone in her voice. 'Your father died. We don't know exactly when. Marianne found him this morning lying on the kitchen floor. She went to look for him as the dialysis clinic had called because he wasn't there for his treatment.'

There was a moment of silence. I tried to imagine the scene that Marianne, a friend of my father who had looked after him since my mother had died, had encountered that morning in our kitchen when she went looking for him. I also tried to figure out in seconds what my father's death would mean to my scheduled trip to Prague. Rosa knew about my plans to travel to Berlin for five days after the dance event and then come to my home town. I guess I was thinking about how to tell her and my relatives in Germany that I would not cancel my trip to Prague, an event which I had worked for in the past eight months and for which

I had paid a substantial amount of money upfront. There would be no refund if I was not attending. And it was a once-in-a-lifetime event I had been looking forward to the whole year.

'Oh no,' I replied eventually, without feeling any emotions. 'I knew that this would happen one day. But I can't come right now. You know that I am flying to Prague on Saturday for a week to attend the dance event. I won't cancel that now. Nothing will change if I come a week later. I will come to Neustadt Sunday in a week.'

My aunt didn't discuss this any further. Partly, I guess, because I said it with such conviction that she accepted it. There was also more important stuff to attend to in this very moment.

'The paramedic needs to talk to you,' she continued. I heard her explaining that she had the daughter of the deceased person on the phone from Australia, and shortly after the voice of a guy repeated what Rosa had already told me:

'Good morning, we found your father lying on the kitchen floor, his head in a pool of blood. We assume he has been lying there for a while. We couldn't do anything for him. My condolences. We now have to wait until his doctor arrives to attest his death.'

'Ok, thank you very much,' I replied still trying to come to terms what I had just learned.

He handed the phone back two Rosa who started to tell me what I would need to do first, namely choosing a company to organise the funeral. There were only a couple of undertakers in our small country town, so I went with the first one she recommended. She went on to name a long list of things I would need to get sorted in the next days before my flight to Europe. Her husband, my uncle, had only passed away the year before and she had gone through the whole process not long ago. I can't remember how long we were on the phone together, constantly interrupted by conversations that were going on at the crime scene. Because there was money lying on the floor next to my father's body, the police was called to investigate the cause of his death. Later on, his doctor attested that he must have had a stroke, lost consciousness and collapsed onto the floor.

While Rosa kept describing what was going on, I tried to imagine all the people in the kitchen, my father's body lying on the floor next to the table, the blood around his head, Euro bills scattered around him. Sitting at my desk in Sydney, 10,000 km away, pulled away from my work projects that I wanted to finish before the end of the week, made the whole scene somehow surreal.

The next four days passed in a flash with the same rhythm. I would get up early, usually around 5am, to get my work and all the preparations for my three-week trip done by 4pm when I would start calling Germany. I spoke almost every day with the funeral company and followed their instructions to get everything ticked off my list in the lead up to the day. As my father wanted to be cremated, there were additional steps to follow. I would spent the remaining hours of the afternoon talking to my aunt or trying to get other jobs done via phone or email.

Twelve days later, I touched down at Frankfurt airport, utterly exhausted from a week of sleep deprivation, but filled up with happiness and joy from my dancing, and caught one of Germany's fast trains to Mannheim where Rosa picked me up from the central station. The last time I had seen her was in May 2018, a few month before my uncle passed away from cancer.

'Hello, how are you?' She asked me when I found her in the pick-up area behind the station. We hugged each other tightly.

'I had the most amazing week ever!' I didn't know where to start telling her about my experiences in Prague.

I stayed at her place where she now lived by herself and we both enjoyed each other's company. Because we had spoken almost daily about the organisation of my father's funeral on the phone in between my dancing events, we didn't talk a lot about it that

Sunday afternoon. I sensed that Rosa was still coming to terms with the loss of my uncle. I even felt his loss when I entered their apartment where many things reminded me of him. He loved art, and one of the last things I had done before I saw him for the last time, was discussing with him how to curate and hang three brick-shaped sculptures on the wall in their living room.

'How are you going, living by yourself?' I asked her.

'I'm ok, I try to make the best of my situation. It is not easy but you have to move forward. Life goes on. And I have Felix and Florian and my grandchildren in Berlin. They help me a lot and we visit each other as often as we can.'

'Thanks so much for all your help with the funeral and everything else that needs to be sorted.' I was so grateful to have Rosa as a family member and friend. I didn't know how I would have coped without her over the years.

My work started the next morning. I had asked my aunt on the day of my father's passing to collect his personal folders with all the paperwork we had to go through to resolve his household. This turned out to be detective work because my father was not very organised in these things. I set up 'my office' on my aunt's dining table surrounded by boxes of folders and bank statements. In the next ten days, I went through all the paperwork, one by one, cancelling subscriptions, his telephone line, the water and electricity supply. In some cases, the only existing paperwork was so old that the telephone numbers weren't connected anymore, and I had to find out who to call to tick this item off my to-do list.

'I can't believe this. All he left me behind is more work!' I sometimes shouted out to my aunt, totally frustrated, when I found another document that triggered a whole series of investigative calls and emails.

On top of that, I had to sell his car and organise a de-cluttering business to empty our family home, which was still full of stuff from all the generations who had lived in our house. No one had ever cared about what they would leave behind for their children to sort out. Feelings of anger and resentment popped up because I had asked my father several times over the past years to get rid of all the old furniture and sorting out the stuff in our attic. He continuously refused to do something about it and all he said was: 'You can do this when I am not here anymore.' What made all of this undertaking even more complicated was the fact that my father had sold our family home. As a result, we had to deal with the new owner every time we wanted to get in.

The day the de-cluttering company arrived to empty the house, I walked through each room for the final time taking a few small pieces that I didn't want to leave to their unknown destiny. Childhood memories forged their way to the surface of my conscious mind. Furniture pieces, paintings, and other memorabilia reminded me of mum, and I wished I could take more things with me to Sydney. I grabbed a few things and put them in a washing basket my aunt had brought: a vintage Monopoly board game that I loved as a child, a candle holder, a couple of original oil paintings by a local artist depicting my father and myself as a toddler. We also rolled up a couple of rugs which I would leave at my aunt's place for the time being. I knew I wouldn't be able to transport them to Sydney, so I offered her to use one in her apartment. We found a nice spot for it and I knew that she would enjoy it, which made me happy. I couldn't thank her enough for all her help in the past ten years since we had left Germany.

To leave my family home on that day knowing that I would not come back made me nostalgic and sad. However, I had said goodbye in 2015 when I had realised that this house was not my home any longer. My life and sons were in Australia and I was looking forward to returning home.

Two days before my return flight to Sydney, we gathered in the small chapel at our local cemetery where my mother had been buried over 20 years ago. My father's black urn, surrounded be a colourful wreath of summer flowers, took centre stage next to a picture of him on a glass table top sitting on a high, column-style base in a greyish cement colour. An installation of green and white hanging plants fell down from the table like a waterfall. Flanked by two grey plant stands with ball-shaped, green hedges. Another hedge ball was sitting on the floor at the base of the high table. There were also two candles in glass cylinders filled with sand and rose petals standing on the floor with a heart-shaped arrangements of tea lights in between. Behind the table, two large Ficus plants and a set of two high candle stands with five candles each arranged on ascending holders complemented the symmetrical arrangement. Red, pink, yellow, and white rose petals were scattered across the floor brightening up the scene.

The chapel filled with old friends of my parents, some of whom I hadn't seen for decades and couldn't remember their names. Some came to me, shook my hand or nodded with their heads in my direction to express their condolences. After the service, we walked down to the lower part of the cemetery where the Council

had created a large grass area for urn graves. These graves had no grave stones but small, square stone plates set into the grass with the name, birth and death dates of the buried person.

We all stood in a semi-circle around the small hole in which his ashes were lowered by two pallbearers. After the priest had said a few words, I was the first to come forward. I spent a moment in silence looking into the small grave while my eyes filled with tears. It dawned on me that I now was an orphan having lost both my parents. There was no reason to come home anymore to this little village where I had grown up. I remembered some of the good times I had spent with my father when I was a young child. There were Sunday afternoon picnic outings, boat trips on the Rhine, and trips to the soccer stadium of our local club who played in the Bundesliga and the Formula 1 race track in Hockenheim. But, unfortunately, there were too many other memories overshadowing the good times. These memories had made me feel angry and helpless. I watched my mother suffering because she had to bear the consequences from my father's often very selfish behaviour. I wished we had had a better relationship when I was a teenager and later in my life. I wished there would have been more and better conversations in our family. After I had finally heard more about his childhood and upbringing three years earlier at his 80th birthday, I knew he had done the best he could with the knowledge that was available to him. And I felt sorry for him that he had spent his whole life in the same house and place. He was a victim of his circumstances and never had the courage to break free and change his life.

I grabbed a handful of rose petals from a bowl that was standing next to the grave and threw them onto his urn. Then, I walked away to take my place again in the semi-circle of family members. Slowly but steadily, all the other mourners went to his grave and either used the rose petals or a shovel of earth to cover the urn and say good-bye to my father. More of my parents' friends came over to me expressing their condolences and telling me their name to make sure I knew who they were. I said thank you and smiled wondering what they were thinking of the daughter who emigrated to Australia and only returned a few times in the past ten years to visit her father. On the other hand, that was what I had chosen and I didn't really bother what everyone thought.

Afterwards, the remaining family members, Mum's brothers and their wives, one of my cousins and his wife and some distant relatives gathered at a local restaurant for the wake with the traditional coffee and cake and some savoury sandwiches. Apart from the usual small talk, cherished memories were exchanged amongst old friends and people asked about my life in Australia. After all, it was a pleasant afternoon and I felt relief that I had sorted out the majority of my father's affairs and only left a few minor things for my aunt to finish in the coming weeks.

The day before my departure I met with my best high school friend, Ulli, a last time. We strolled through the cemetery and visited all the graves of the relatives we had already lost: both my grandmothers, my mother, two of her brothers, my father, and my friend's mother. We sat down at a bench next to my father's urn grave enjoying the beautiful views over the Rhine plains. We had known each other for almost 45 years and there was a mutual understanding without words. After a moment of silence, without changing the gaze to the horizon, she said:

'You know what, I believe this is how your father wanted to die. He didn't want to go into aged care, he knew that he would not be able to live by himself much longer, and he knew that you were coming.'

Nothing else needed to be said. I had had a similar conversation with my aunt.

'I think you're right,' I replied eventually.

On the plane home, I felt a heavy weight lifted from my shoulders. I didn't have to worry about my father any longer from the other side of the world, and another chapter of my life was closed.

CROSSROADS

"It is not impermanence that makes us suffer. What makes us suffer is wanting things to be permanent when they are not."

Thich Nhat Hanh

*****

In my first lesson after Daniele's return from Europe in early October 2019, we discussed my results from Prague. Overall, I was very happy and proud of my achievements. For the majority of my dances, I got Silver or Gold results and made the 6th place in the final of the All Round Championship. A proof that persistence, being open to growth, and pushing through the hard times in my lessons paid off.

I was especially delighted about the feedback for my solo routine from three international judges. They rated me Silver, the second highest in the competition, and pointed out my precise technique, footwork and posture. One wrote: "Very sensual and elegant on the floor. Bravo!" Another said: "You are a natural in this dance, well done!"

Daniele and I resumed our lessons as usual to prepare for the final event of the year, our studio's showcase in Sydney Tattersall's Club at the end of November.

Reflecting on the past eleven months, I was proud of my achievements. I had reached all my dancing goals. With Daniele by my side, I mastered my first solo routine in Argentine Tango and performed it three times successfully in two showcases and finally in Prague. I improved my Smooth dances significantly, and I completed my Bronze 3 exam successfully to advance to Bronze 4 at the end of September.

All was good in my dancing world except for this nagging feeling in my body that something would change in the foreseeable future. Daniele and I had had several conversations over the time we worked together about what he wanted to achieve in life and the progression of his career as a dance instructor. And I knew that one day he was going to say good bye.

That day came sooner than expected. After my last lesson before Christmas, the studio owner informed me that Daniele was going to leave Arthur Murray to open his own dance school together with his now fiancé who was also a dancer. The moment the words were spoken, I burst into tears. Everything I had planned for 2020 had crashed within a second like a house of cards. Someone had just pulled the carpet under my feet. I composed myself while the studio owner tried to embellish the bad news, although I could hear the desperation in her voice. She was about to lose the one teacher who had the most students across her two dance studios.

In a state of shock I changed my shoes, packed my bags and left with a forced smile on my face. Would I ever dance with Daniele again? My heart was aching and thoughts tumbled through my mind trying to make sense of what I had just heard. I ended up sitting in the bus, on the upper floor, as usual, and couldn't hold back the tears. Silently, I cried for the entire trip to the Northern Beaches. What would happen with my dancing? Would I ever see Daniele again? Who would be my new instructor? Would I still go to Athens in 2020? Too many questions without answers, and all I felt was sadness and devastation.

I spent the next days and nights in a state of mourning. The mere thought of not being able to dance with Daniele again made me cry. A friend and life coach tried to console me: "Let your emotions emerge and take the time to mourn, this loss is like a relationship breakup, and it hurts. The more you acknowledge your feelings, the quicker your brain will let go of them."

Every morning, in my mediation, I prayed for a sign from the Universe that I would see him again; that his new school would not be too far away, so that I could still have lessons with him. The studio's Christmas party was only a week away. It would be Daniele's farewell evening and the last chance to have a few dances with him. I was contemplating about not going, as I was not sure how I would manage to not start crying again during the evening.

The day came, and, of course, I went. I danced Salsa and Bachata with him, two of my favourite Street Latin dances, and bathed in a feeling of gratitude to have had him as teacher for 15 months. I managed to survive the evening without tears knowing that I was not the only one missing him. At one time, all of his students were sitting in one row on the chairs around the dance floor, pretending to cry while passing a tissue box around. We all could feel the sadness and tried to cope somehow.

Then, the time had come. Daniele gave each of us a big hug and wished us well. Before he left, I asked him again where his new dance school would be. 'Sorry, Bettina, I can't tell you now, but you will find out anyway.' He turned around the last time, waving at me, and disappeared into the hallway outside the studio door.

I felt again that tightness in my tummy and swallowed my tears. Although the party wasn't finished, it was over for me. Not long after, I packed my bag and left. My body felt hollow and empty.

My dancing journey had also become a topic of conversation with my teenage sons. When they stayed with me, I regularly informed them what was going on in my dancing world. Although they never talked a lot, I knew that they are watching, even it was only on Instagram. They were curious to hear about my experiences, my upcoming competitions, and my plans for the future.

In 2019, when I was training for Prague almost every day of the week, Max would often ask me whether I would go dancing in the evening. The boys adapted quickly that we had dinner earlier and that I wasn't always home to eat with them. They both accepted my passion for my new hobby and the sacrifices that come with it knowing how much it meant to me. When I had told them with sadness about Daniele leaving the dance school, Max asked:

'What are you going to do now? Are you going to his new school?'

'I don't know yet where his new school will be but I will try and keep having lessons with him,' I replied. And my son nodded in agreement.

As the studio was closed for a couple of weeks over Christmas, I had plenty of time to succumb to whatever feelings arose and also think about what I would do with my dancing in 2020. I didn't know yet where I would head but I looked into the future with an open mind and curiosity.

There was only one other teacher, who had joined the studio in April 2019, who I could see myself dancing with. I didn't know him very well, as I only had danced with him at socials from time to time. I had never had a private lesson. However, he was the only instructor who was tall enough for me.

In January 2020, the start of a new decade and after two years with Arthur Murray, my gut feeling signalled that I had come to a crossroad with my dancing and that exciting things were going to happen this year. What did the Universe have in store for me? Where would I go? What would I do? With whom would I dance? Questions I asked in my daily meditation. I trusted in the Universe which usually has far greater plans for us than we can ever imagine. I also consulted my Tarot card deck and was not at all surprised to draw a card that announced "Winds of change are blowing, events will occur with great speed, and the Go-Getter is unstoppable."

Shortly before New Year's Eve, I saw on Instagram that Daniele and his fiancé would open their new dance school in Arncliffe, near the airport in Sydney's South, in February. I was over the moon! A trip to the airport was still doable and much better than what I had anticipated. I messaged him that I wanted to keep having lessons with him, even if it was only once a week.

Not long, and the Universe started sending me signs answering the many questions that kept my mind occupied. First, I reconnected with a former Arthur Murray student, who had left the studio shortly after I joined to pursue a new venture in International Ballroom. I met her over a cup of tea to learn more about her experiences dancing competitions. Afterwards, I felt that going down this avenue was something I wanted to explore further. After more research into the industry and becoming a member of DanceSport Australia, I decided to leave the Arthur Murray at the end of April 2020 and find a Professional partner to dance International Ballroom & Latin competitions with me.

Mid-February, I made my way to Arncliffe to have my very first lesson with Daniele in his new studio. It was a happy reunion after two months, and the moment we started dancing waltz, I felt like coming home. When I asked him whether he would consider dancing competitions with me, he explained that he wanted to concentrate on growing his new school for the time being and not enter the competition world again at this stage.

 Back at Arthur Murray, in one of our group classes, we learned some steps in International Rumba, which is very different to the American style Rumba the school taught. Similar to when I first learned the Argentine Tango, I was instantly intrigued by the sensuality and sophistication of this dance. At the same time, I realised how challenging the technique was. But I was usually up for a challenge in my dancing and asked my new instructor to teach me more steps in International Rumba in my private lessons. The following weekend, I decided spontaneously to go to a Saturday group class, which I hadn't attended for a while. I couldn't believe when the instructor announced that we would keep working on International Rumba technique for the next three weeks. My decision to explore the International Ballroom scene in the new decade was reinforced.

I kept my plans secret for a while, wondering when it was the best time to tell my teacher and the studio. One evening, after my lesson, I felt it was the right time to reveal my plans.

'I feel I have come to a crossroad with my dancing,' I started. 'I really enjoyed the two years with Arthur Murray, especially last year dancing in Prague. And since Daniele left, I have been contemplating about what I want to do with my dancing in the future. I love the International style and am up for a new challenge with international competitions.'

'So you're going to leave?'

'Yes.'

'Are you looking for a Pro partner then?' he continued after a moment of silence.

'Yes.'

What I didn't expect that night was that not only my dancing journey, but also the whole world would be shaken to its core a few weeks later with the COVID19 pandemic hitting with unforeseen vengeance.

COMING HOME

"The journey between who you once were, and who you are now becoming, is where the dance of life really takes place."

Barbara de Angelis, Relationship Consultant, Author

*****

On the 23rd March 2020, the dance schools in Australia closed their doors leaving teachers without work and students without a space to practise. Within a few hours, my social life was erased from my calendar. As our country went into lockdown, I had to come to terms with the fact that I wouldn't be dancing in the foreseeable future and that no one knew when we would return to some kind of normality.

The days merged with each other, seamlessly, with no beginning and no end. A continuous flow that carried me along. Only interrupted by the anchors I put in place: my morning routine, my lunchtime walk, and my evening routine watching the news at 6:30pm. On day two of staying at home, I felt that I had been in isolation for weeks. I turned towards online yoga to get some exercise apart from walking.

After the first week in lockdown, the days seemed to pass quicker as I got used to my new normal. Except that I started to miss my dancing more and more. I realised that I would lose at least six months of preparing my transition to the International Ballroom circus. I felt like hanging in limbo between the dance school where I was still enrolled and my new venture into an exciting new world of dancing. I started practicing some steps and technique at home, following instructions on short videos, however, it was not the same as dancing with a partner. The first three weeks without dancing felt like eternity, and there was no sign in sight that we would resume our passion in the near future.

DanceSport Australia had cancelled all events until September. And I felt more and more restless. I needed to find an outdoor space where I could have lessons with my teacher.

I googled a few outdoor spaces and we agreed to meet on a Sunday morning at a park nearby his home for a first outdoor technique lesson. We couldn't believe our eyes when we saw a shaded, square verandah in front of a kiosk, which had been closed. The terrace was elevated from the oval and framed by trees on one side, which gave us some sort of privacy. It was almost too good to be true!

We resumed our practice and kept working on my Latin routines: Rumba, Samba, and ChaCha. The fact that we couldn't touch each other was challenging but also had a positive side. It forced me to focus more on my technique, steps, and the directions in relation to my dance partner and the audience. From this day on, we returned once a week to our new outdoor dance studio where I even started learning a new dance: the Jive. Where there is a will, there's a way.

Jive was one of the three new dances of the International Ballroom syllabus that I needed to master for the competitions apart from Quickstep and Paso Doble. All of them challenging in their own right. In contrast to American Ballroom, International Ballroom focuses on choreographed routines rather than freestyle dancing. The advantage was that, as the follower, I knew which steps we were going to dance in our competitions. The challenge, however, was to perform the routine on the day without mistakes. Especially in the speedy Latin dances, one wrong step could throw you totally out of the game. The trick to mastery was repetition, over and over again, until the muscle memory is established.

By mid-May, I finally closed my chapter with Arthur Murray and informed Daniele about it. He replied with a lovely text message:

'Although it might be a bitter-sweet moment for you leaving the dance school, the next chapter of your dancing journey will be exciting. We are looking forward to seeing you again and I can't wait to have you back in our new studio.'

After almost two months in lockdown, one of my former female instructors from the dance school started giving outdoor lessons on Council grounds on the Northern Beaches. I loved the workout and finally dancing some ballroom steps again after weeks of practising my Latin dances. We had a ball dancing Foxtrot and Tango without a partner on the netball courts among many other groups of fitness enthusiasts who met there on a Saturday morning.

In July, the dance schools were finally allowed to reopen, and I returned to Arncliffe for one double lesson a week with Daniele to practise my Ballroom dances Waltz, Tango, and Foxtrot, which I started missing.

'Can't you dance the Waltz routine with me at the Canberra event next year?' I asked him again.

'We are planning to go to Canberra and some other competitions,' he admitted.

'That's great! So I can dance at least the Waltz with you there,' I exclaimed, content about my small step forward.

One Sunday in early August, I messaged Daniele to tell him that I would like to start learning routines in the other ballroom dances to be better prepared when the competitions would be resumed. When I arrived for my lesson the next day, Daniele greeted me with the words:

'I need to talk to you.'

'Sure, what about?'

'Look, I know I said to you when we opened the school that I didn't want to go back to International, which is what I grew up with. Our goal is to grow our dance school. But things have changed, and I know that you are looking for someone to dance the ballroom dances with you, so I decided to do it. It's a big commitment, and I am excited to embark on this journey with you and want to make sure that I get the same commitment from you, which means that you would need to come in more often for practise. I also wanted to ask you if you were willing to dance all ten dances with me, Ballroom and Latin.'

I couldn't believe what I had heard. I was over the moon! To dance with Daniele at competitions was a dream come true! Listening to my heart, I knew the answer.

'Oh my God, this is so exciting! Thanks so much for doing this for me! I would love to dance with you!'

That day, I left the dance school as the happiest girl on the planet. In the car on my way home, I reflected on my dance journey during the lockdown and the partnership with my Arthur Murray instructor, which had become challenging in recent weeks. He often threw me into the deep end with advanced step combinations and moves, and although I was eager to try everything, I sometimes became totally frustrated when he repeatedly said that I was too slow and out of time. In one of our last lessons we clashed about his way of teaching. Since that day a voice inside me had become louder and louder questioning whether he was the right partner for me. At the same time, I knew that Daniele would never talk to me like that. And the thought of my partner getting angry with me during competitions was something I didn't want to explore further and made the decision to end our partnership.

I knew that I was in best hands with Daniele. His commitment to our new venture and his excitement about this new chapter in our dancing journey was contagious. We often made jokes when the lessons were particularly challenging, and he would look at me and sigh: 'Oh dear, what have we got ourselves into?' Then, we resumed the practice. In one of my lessons, I revealed that 'it felt like coming home' when I was dancing with him. 'Thank you,' he replied with a smile.

In the meantime, DanceSport Australia had announced that most likely there wouldn't be any events before March 2021, which meant that we had six months to get ready for our first competition. My lessons had become a whole new purpose, as I knew what I was working for. I made plans which of the bigger competitions in 2021 I would like to attend, including ASDAC The Outback Crown in Canberra, and the Tasmanian Open in Launceston, both in August.

'Are you planning to go away next year?' I asked him one day.

'Why?'

'I want to plan my dancing year as early as possible, in the beginning of January and need to know for which competitions you are around.'

'We are not going anywhere next year,' he replied.

Our plan was to practise at some of the smaller competitions around Sydney. To say that I was excited about the next 18 months was an understatement! I resumed three double lessons a week and we alternated Ballroom and Latin to progress with all the routines at the same time. Plus, I had to learn two new dances: Quickstep and Paso Doble. Once I remembered the routines, we started focusing on the technique and arm styling. Lastly, Daniele told me we would have so-called stamina lessons, which means we would dance all the five Ballroom and Latin dances one after the other as it is required during a competition.

I was at the dance school on Mondays, Wednesdays, and Fridays, and my work and private life revolved around my lessons. I noticed the more I danced, the happier I was!

DRESS REHEARSAL

"To watch us dance is to hear our hearts speak."

Hopi Indian Tribe Saying

*****

'I want to learn The Fleckerl,' I kept insisting.

Our heads together, we were both looking at one of my saved Instagram videos on my phone. The Fleckerl was one of the most difficult steps in the International Ballroom syllabus for Viennese Waltz.

'Please show me how it is done,' I didn't give up. Daniele always preferred to get the basic stuff right first before moving on to more advanced steps.

'Ok, let's see how we go,' he rolled his eyes, and started to show me the steps in slow motion. I soon realised that he was right. The trick with The Fleckerl is to dance it very neat and tight while spinning on the spot and never losing the upper body frame.

We practised the steps in each of our Ballroom lessons, and I had to admit that it was much harder than I thought it would be. My steps were too big and I was often out of time. I started questioning myself whether it was a wise move to keep insisting on dancing it at the upcoming Grading Day, a dance event organised by another studio.

One day, Daniele put four chairs in a square in the middle of the dance floor. The legs of the chairs were almost touching each other. Then, he stepped into the small space between the chairs and demonstrated how to dance The Fleckerl on his own. Without touching the chair legs, of course! Then, it was my turn. I stepped into the tiny square space, and started the step sequence. It took a couple of steps and my foot banged against one of the chair legs. So, I had to start again.

Sometimes, I wondered whether I was asking too much of myself, at the same time, I was prepared to do whatever it took to improve my dancing. And I knew I needed to master this step combination for the competitions in 2021.

'We are participating in a dance showcase organised by Move With Me in Castle Hill. Are you interested to go? We could use it to practise our new routines and to get some feedback from the judges,' he pointed at a poster on the window one day.

I read that the Grading Day & Soirée 2020 was scheduled in the Woodcroft Neighbourhood Centre on the 8th November. It was a dance showcase of independent dance schools giving students the opportunity to perform their dancing in American style Smooth and Rhythm plus some Speciality dances, such as Bolero, Bachata, Salsa, Mambo and Hustle. In the evening, there would be a light dinner and social dancing until 9:30 pm.

I didn't have to read the event description twice and made the decision on the spot that I would participate in this one and only event in 2020. Not only would it be a great opportunity to receive feedback from three judges at the first and most probably only dance event in 2020, but also to prove myself and Daniele how much I had improved since Prague and that it was the right decision to dance competitions in the future. And finally, it was time to get those glamorous dance dresses out of the wardrobe again!

How I had missed wearing them! It was in November 2019 that we had the last Arthur Murray showcase before lockdown. I was looking forward to floating across the floor with my stunning black and gold ballroom gown, which I had found a year before at the house of the seamstress who I had met through the dance school. As she happened to live close-by, I had her alter one of my Latin dresses for the event in Prague. During one of the fittings, I saw the black beauty hanging in her living room.

'Wow, whose dress is this?' I couldn't suppress my excitement.

'That's for sale,' Rebecca replied.

'Can I try it on?'

'Yes, sure.'

I slipped into the dress and it fitted perfectly. It seemed to be made for me!

'How much is it?' I wanted to know.

'I'll have to chat to the owner and get back to you.'

A few days later, the gorgeous ballroom gown was mine. The body part is covered in black and silver diamantes, artistically placed in floral patterns and swirls. A black, floaty and multi-layered chiffon skirt with a white underlay swings elegantly around my legs when dancing the Waltz, Foxtrot, and Tango. It is timeless and elegant. One of my favourite ballroom outfits!

In anticipation of dancing my International Rumba routine, I asked Rebecca to custom-make me an elegant dress to suit the Rumba, which is a very sensual and sophisticated dance. I found a few example dresses online and she drew a design according to my brief. We agreed that she would have the new dress ready for the grading day.

A couple of weeks before the event, I said to Daniele:

'I would like to bring in my dresses to have a rehearsal in them. I haven't worn them for a year and don't want to wear them on the day for the first time again. And I also want you to have a look at the new dress, which I had made for the Rumba in particular. I am not sure if it is suitable for the Cha Cha and the Jive. It is quite elegant. I would like to hear your opinion.'

'Sure, no problem. Bring them in.'

I remembered the year before when Daniele had told me that he had sent students off the dance floor to get changed more than once when they had appeared in inappropriate dresses at showcases. We all used to do dress rehearsals at Arthur Murray to get used to dancing in the competition gowns. I didn't believe it at first but it felt very different to dance in the competition outfits, especially in the long ballroom dresses. In fact, the dresses are part of the excitement around ballroom dancing. It just feels so special to wear them!

The week before the event, I brought my gowns to the dance school to have a rehearsal in them. It was exciting to wear and dance in them again. And Daniele gave me a thumbs up for my new Latin dress.

Finally, three days before the event, we got our heat lists and the times when we would be dancing. Although it was only a grading day in a very social atmosphere, I felt a funny feeling in my stomach, a typical sign that I was nervous. The fact that a friend and her husband wanted to pop by for a couple of hours to watch me dancing didn't ease the tension.

As usual with dance events, the day started early with a new hairstylist, who I had found in a local Facebook group, coming to my home at 7:30 am on Sunday morning. I had to be ready with my makeup on before she arrived.

Afterwards, I had a protein shake for breakfast, as I never could eat a lot on those dance event days, and packed the last items in my small suitcase before the hairdresser arrived. It took her 45 minutes to create a ballroom hairstyle that would keep in place for the day and evening event.

Everything went to plan. At 8:20 am, I loaded my suitcase and two large clothing bags, one protecting my ballroom dress, the other one covering two Latin dresses and one of my favourite

Tango dresses for the Soiree, into the car. According to my navigation system, the drive to Woodcroft was 50 minutes.

I arrived early and found a park right in front of the Neighbourhood Centre, which was located in a parkland surrounded by a residential area. The back of the event space opened to a timber terrace overlooking a large lake populated with ducks and birds and surrounded by trees and grass. The morning sun embellished the beautiful setting. I was looking forward to my day of dancing!

Not long after my arrival, Daniele and another student pulled into the carpark. The dancing happened in the main event space, which was a rectangular, light-filled room with large windows on two sides and a small kitchen on the opposite wall. Due to the lack of change rooms, we used the kitchen that was not in use that day as a storage room.

The bathrooms, which we had to use as change rooms, were located in the entrance hall and someone had kindly brought a couple of racks where we could hang up our large clothing bags. As we were still early, the official start was at 10:15 am, I disappeared into one of the toilet cubicles and changed into my ballroom gown.

In the next half an hour, the event space filled with more and more people in colourful, sparkly ballroom dresses. The excitement of finally being back at a dance event, the first one in 2020, was permeating the room.

'Oh my God, I have to dance the first heat,' a young girl next to me confessed with a nervous smile on her face.

'You will be fine,' I said to her. 'I'm freaking out, too.'

My first heat was number 24, the Waltz, and the churning in my stomach grew by the minute. The day before, I spoke to one of my dancer friends from Arthur Murray and had told her how nervous I was.

'What are you nervous about?' She asked. 'You danced a solo routine in Prague in front of 250 people!'

'I know! I guess, it's because we haven't danced at an event for so long, and I just need to get used to it again.

When heat 24 came up, I tried to calm myself down with breathing exercises. Daniele and I were standing on the side of the dance floor ready to go. He held my left hand, which somehow relaxed me a bit. 'You will be fine', he kept repeating. 'You know your stuff.'

I know that it was only me who put pressure on myself. I had worked very hard over the past three months and I didn't want to let him down. Not after he made the commitment to dance competitions with me in 2021. I wanted him to be proud of me.

'Heat number 24, the Waltz. Please welcome Bettina and Daniele to the floor.

I took a deep breath and walked on Daniele's side to the other side of the dance floor where we had agreed to start our routine. The ballroom routines were choreographed to maximise the use of the floor and the corners for specific step combinations.

When the music started, I could feel the tightness in my body. It was still challenging for me to remember the steps, the proper technique, stay in my frame, and make it look effortlessly. When I saw some of my videos afterwards, I noticed that I definitely needed to improve my facial expression and smile more!

After a few steps, I succumbed to Daniele's lead and relaxed a bit more. I finished my Waltz without major hiccups. When we left the floor, Daniele whispered: 'Well done, I am proud of you.'

Next up was the Tango and the Foxtrot, which I danced with other couples on the floor. Both heats went well and I only made some minor mistakes, which were hardly visible for the audience who kept cheering the dancers on.

My last ballroom heat, the Viennese Waltz, was also the final heat for the ballroom event. Viennese is one of the most difficult dances, and we were the only couple on the dance floor. Our routine included The Fleckerl, which we had practised over and over again. Because of my persistence, Daniele agreed to include it but in a moderate version – why would we want to make our lives harder, he used to joke. He always made sure that I looked good on the floor "because the judges would instantly see when a step was too advanced for my level of dancing." As usual, I appreciated and trusted his advice.

When the organiser called us to the floor, I knew The Fleckerl was coming up right at the beginning of our routine after a couple of turns when Daniele would lead me into a contra check. I concentrated hard to listen to the rhythmic beat of the Viennese Waltz and not to stuff up the step into it. To my delight, I managed to dance The Fleckerl without mistakes and we kept spinning around the dance floor until the music stopped. The crowd applauded and Daniele repeated that I had been doing very well with all my ballroom routines. I was very happy to have mastered the first part of the day and well aware that the next challenges would come up after lunch with the Latin routines and especially the Jive when we would again be the only couple on the floor.

As we were behind schedule, the lunch break was short and I only had a bite of my protein bar, as I never have an appetite at dance events. My first Rhythm heat was the Rumba, followed by the ChaCha, the Jive, and the Bolero.

We danced American style Rumba, as the beat for International Rumba is much slower than American style and doesn't fit the music. The Rumba went well, and so did the ChaCha. I was very happy with my performance dancing my routine without major mistakes. Next up was the Jive. Despite my nervousness, I felt quite confident in this routine. I even managed to put on a good show, adding a cheeky facial expression to my steps. The last dance of the rhythm section was the Bolero, one of my favourite dances and not a choreographed routine. The Bolero has the same beat as International Rumba and I loved dancing it in my new ivory-coloured flowing dress. It suited the dance perfectly.

Afterwards, I became more relaxed because the remaining heats were all the fun Club dances: Salsa, Bachata, and Hustle.

Overall, I was very pleased with my performances let alone the compliments from other dancers about my dancing and dresses. One lady even asked me for the number of the seamstress who had made my Latin dress.

The day concluded with a light dinner and a social dancing night. As if we hadn't danced enough during the day! At 9:30 pm, after a 15-hour day, we finally said goodbye and I sat in my car for another hour on my way home.

I was so tired that I drove home on autopilot, not faster than 80km/h while cars and trucks overtook me. My mind replayed the day dance-by-dance, mentally and physically exhausted but happy and content. How had the judges rated my dancing? Would they consider that I had danced The Fleckerl? I knew we would have to wait a couple of weeks until the results would be sent to the dance school, so patience was required. I was curious to read the judges' comments, which would be valuable feedback to work on until the our first competition in 2021.

Three weeks later, at our weekend Samba workshop, Daniele mentioned: 'I got your results. Let's go through the Ballroom dances on Monday!' I scanned the pages and was pleased with what I read. For all my dances I got A and B marks pointing out excellent footwork, beautiful arm styling, great timing and presentation. Suggested improvements for the Ballroom dances were mainly about connection to the floor, more posture extension, better head position, and connection with Daniele. For the Latin dances, the judges asked for more movement in ribcage, more Cuban motion, which is the hip movement, more use of the front of the ankles, and keeping the feet connected to the floor all the time.

Overall, we had reached our goal to practise our routines in front of an audience and get some feedback. And there was still lots to work on until we would appear as ProAm couple at competition for the first time. I tried not to think too much about it, as it scared the hell out of me.

HOPE IS THE CONDUIT FOR MIRACLES

"Ask and it will be given to you; seek and you will find; knock and the door will be opened to you."

Matthew 7:7

*****

On the 12th January, we finally registered as ProAm couple with DanceSport Australia (DSA). On the 17th January, the entries for the first competition of 2021 in Marrickville would close. We had registered for four dances in the Ballroom event (Waltz, Foxtrot, Tango, and Quickstep) and four dances in the Latin event (Samba, ChaCha, Rumba, and Jive).

When I entered the studio the next day, Daniele grinned at me with a cheeky smile:

'Now, the countdown is on!'

'Don't tell me about it,' I was wondering whether I would be as nervous as at the showcase in November.

We started finishing the Quickstep routine, which was the newest dance for me to learn. I felt the training stepped up another notch that day. At my next lesson, we discussed a new weekly routine to help me learn the Ballroom and Latin dances faster: instead of alternating each lesson between Ballroom and Latin, we wanted to try one week of Ballroom and one week of Latin immersion. I noticed that it was more efficient to spend three double lessons on one style and the next three on the other.

Then, something unexpected happened. On the morning of the 20th January, I woke up to the following text messages from two dancer friends:

"Darn comp postponed," and "Postponed…but that's better than cancelled!"

I didn't believe my eyes and sank back onto my bed staring on my phone in disbelief.

In the next couple of hours, text messages shot back and forth trying to come to terms with the unchangeable. My friend tried to console me with the next competition coming up one month later, at the end of March. However, it turned out that this event only allowed Teacher-Student entries, which Daniele and I couldn't dance, as he still didn't have the required accreditation from DSA. It took me the whole day to digest that Marrickville and Beecroft were not going to happen.

I knew that asking 'why' would not bring any relief nor an answer. I reminded me of what I had learned in my Neuro Linguistic Programming training in 2019, namely to ask better questions.

What could I learn from this?

How could I find beauty in this situation?

When I had my online Pilates session that morning with my teacher being stuck in continuous lockdown in London, I realised how lucky I was living in Sydney and being able to get out and about my daily life including the dance school. Maybe it was a sign from the Universe that I was not yet ready and needed to practice more. I decided to not take my foot of the accelerator but keep up my practice as if the competition was on, as there would be another event coming up sooner or later.

I cancelled my spray tan appointment and the hairstylist but didn't tell my seamstress, who I was going to see for a fitting at the end of January what had happened. She was altering my black Latin dress, which I had worn at my very first showcase in Leichhardt and which I had decided would be fabulous 'new' Samba outfit. I never really liked the halter neck and we had agreed that she would cut it off and change the dress into an asymmetrical design with several straps running diagonally from one of my shoulders down the back.

At my last visit, I had also brought her a second-hand Ballroom gown that I had purchased off a woman in Sydney's Hills District early 2018 for $350. It was lavender with numerous diamantes of various sizes in purple, blue-green, and transparent embellishing the dress like a stream of water flowing from the neckline, to the back and down to the skirt where they merged into a border of lavender feathers decorating the seam of the skirt.

I had bought it because of the colour and the feathers neglecting that it didn't fit properly. And because it had two layers on top of the body suit and was decorated with many stones, it became very heavy when dancing in it. Plus, I got very quickly very sweaty under the thick material. Not a comfortable feeling.

I hadn't worn it since June 2018 and was considering selling it or throwing it out. But something inside me told me to take it to Rebecca to hear whether she would be able to alter and revive it somehow. At least, I thought, I keep all the stones, which could be easily recycled on a new dress. At my next visit, I carried the heavy clothing bag to Rebecca's house. To get a better idea how it looked on me, she asked me to wear it. I slipped into it and pulled the heavy fabric over my shoulder.

When she closed the little zipper at the back, she exclaimed:

'Oh my God, this is a June design!'

'A what?'

'This dress is from a very famous designer in Melbourne who used to make all the outfits for Dancing with the Stars. She is out of business now, but her dresses were several thousand dollars, some of them four to five thousand. So we are definitely not throwing this one out!'

'What? And I bought it for $350! What a bargain!'

At that moment, I was glad that I had relied again on my intuition.

We discussed how Rebecca could alter the dress so that it would fit my body shape better and at the same time make it lighter and easier to wear. I asked her to sew a new body suit and take out the second layer above the skirt. We would only need one layer underneath the skirt to keep the volume. We also decided to cut off the sleeves. At my next visit, I would try it on to see what I think.

'We can always put the sleeves back on,' Rebecca assured me.

I was super excited that I would now get two 'recycled' dresses that would fit me perfectly.

A few days later, I had come to terms that we would not dance in Marrickville, I heard from another dancer who was the Amateur partner of the studio owner who organised the Beecroft competition that there was a slight chance they would consider a ProAm event this year.

I instantly asked her whether it would make sense that I contact him to explain my situation and that it would be much appreciated if he would give this a thought. In the meantime, another dancer told me that she had also spoken with the organiser of the Beecroft event and asked whether they would add ProAm. So I emailed the studio, introduced myself and asked the same question.

A day later, I got a message from my friend:

'They included a ProAm event for both Ballroom and Latin in the comp, three dances each, so we'll dance together in both. Ballroom will be Waltz, Foxtrot, Quickstep, and Latin will be Samba, ChaCha, Rumba.'

'OMG, I emailed them yesterday,' I messaged back.

'They rang me today to ask about you,' she replied.

I instantly conveyed the good news to Daniele and thought that if I had not asked, we would not have been able to dance there.

A few days later, another big competition in Melbourne was cancelled due to Covid19.

In the meantime, I picked up my revived black Latin dress from Rebecca. It looked stunning and finally fitted my body perfectly.

I knew I would wear it at the first occasion we would be able to dance Samba.

We kept practising as if nothing had happened hoping that not more events would be wiped off the DSA calendar. Daniele also came up with a strategic plan how to use my lessons most efficiently to learn the routines and the required technique in parallel. This was a constant challenge, as I had to do everything in parallel.

'Don't be too hard on yourself,' Daniele used to say when I showed signs of frustration because I had forgotten my steps or didn't seem to make any progress with my technique for all the dances I was practising.

'It takes the professionals years of practice to get the Ballroom and Latin technique into their muscle memory. And only then, they start working on their routines. You do everything at the same time, which is challenging. And you're doing well.'

I appreciated his words of solace and knew that I would have to be more patient with my progress. Still, it was challenging as I knew I wouldn't get younger and had probably another ten years of dancing before me if I managed to stay fit and healthy. I could feel that my dancing took its toll on my body already and had started with ongoing 'maintenance,' such as Epsom salt baths to relax my muscles after strenuous lessons and regular chiropractor visits 'to fix' any imbalances in my hips, legs, and back.

'I hope some of the cancelled comps will pop up later this year, which would be a nice surprise,' I said to Daniele in mid-February. At this stage, we had the Beecroft competition as our next goal, which would be danced in practice wear because of Covid restrictions. I was still looking forward to it, however, it was only half the fun if I couldn't show up in my glamorous ballroom gowns.

Then, on Valentine's Day 2021, I found the announcement from the Australian Dancing Society, NSW branch, that their State

Super Spectacular competition would be on in Marrickville on the 18th of April. I was beyond excited and couldn't wait to get to the dance school the next day to discuss with Daniele how we would need to adapt our training, as this competition required us to do four ballroom dances (Waltz, Tango, Foxtrot, and Quickstep) and four Latin dances (Samba, ChaCha, Rumba, and Jive). We had stopped focusing on Tango and Jive, as these dances were not included in the Beecroft comp. But because Marrickville was only four weeks after Beecroft, we would need to work out a plan how to get on top of my Tango and Jive routines straight after the Beecroft event.

About three weeks before the Beecroft event, I experienced a sharp pain in the lower back which wouldn't go away. I ended up at a specialised clinic for sports injuries and saw a physiotherapist twice a week. The constant pain was tiring physically and mentally but the good news was that the physiotherapist didn't ask me to refrain from dancing instead encouraged me to move, go for walks and attend my dance lessons if we could work around the pain. Luckily, there were many things you could practice from technique to arm styling, which didn't put any pressure on my lower back.

There were times in the lead up to the comp where I was not sure whether I could participate. I kept seeing the physiotherapist, booked an appointment with an energy healer and prayed to the Universe daily to make it happen. Even if I was not able to give 100 per cent, I wanted to participate to get used to performing again and prepare myself for the bigger events that we were planning to attend in 2021.

A week before the event, the schedule was published. Daniele and I would only need to be at the venue in the afternoon with our Latin dances starting at 4:45 pm and the Ballroom dances at 6:15 pm. At first sight, it looked like we would be dancing as the only couple on the floor in my age category Masters II. I tried to calm down by telling myself that it would just be another performance in front of a larger audience.

FAKE IT UNTIL YOU MAKE IT

"When we dance, there are no rules. We must be open to whatever song comes on. We have strengths and weaknesses. We might fall or hesitate over our next move, ... but we keep flowing, allowing ourselves to be messy and beautiful."

Jay Shetty, Think Like a Monk

*****

With the help of my Physio and two sessions per week focusing on pain management, I was able to dance the competition on the 27th February despite the fact that I didn't feel fully recovered. I was determined to make it happen no matter what. I was also wondering whether I would be similarly nervous as in November the year before when we danced at the Grading Day.

As it turned out on the day, Daniele and I were not dancing alone in my age group, as the organiser had merged the Masters I (35 to 50 years) and Masters II (51 to 60 years) events. I was relieved to say the least! I found it always nerve-wracking to dance as the only couple on the huge floor with all eyes directed to us. Due to Covid restrictions, the organiser had asked to show up and dance in practice wear. So I didn't bother to get a spray tan or professional hairstyle done. Tons of hairspray and a pony tail did the trick. For my Latin dances, I chose a simple and elegant black dress in a stretch fabric. For the ballroom event, I wore my black practice skirt with a black lace top.

I met Daniele at 3pm in the entrance hall of the Roselea Community Centre to register and pick up our number: 202. The competition was in full swing, with the adult rounds starting. We joined another dancer friend of mine at one of the tables around the dance floor and settled in.

The energy in the Community Centre was electric! The spectators were either sitting around the tables that framed the dance floor or standing along the walls. Couples were practicing their upcoming dances, coaches tried to keep their students' nerves at bay with encouraging words. The dancers who were next lined up at the side of the dance floor, holding hands, and nervously stepping from one foot to the other. The only thing that was missing was the glitz and glamour of the ballroom gowns, which had to stay packed away because of Covid. However, these regulations didn't prevent the ladies from having their hair and makeup done. The smell of perfume and hair spray permeated the air. Everyone seemed to be excited to be able to return to the dance floor after a year-long break.

'Let's go through our routines to warm up,' Daniele suggested.

'Sure, good idea.'

We practiced our Latin routines in the entrance area, which was the only place for the dancers to warm up. I realised that I felt less nervous than I had expected after an hour meditating and visualising a successful day the evening before.

Back in the ballroom, we followed the live schedule and kept watching the other dancers. My lower back pain made me stand up regularly, as I couldn't sit for very long. So I made the best of it and did some leg and feet warm up exercises in a corner of the hall. When it was our turn, Daniele and I walked to the other side of the dance floor where all the couples lined up for their heats.

I took a few deep breaths and told myself that I would give my best no matter what. When we were called on the floor, Daniele gave me his right hand and led me right o the middle. I smiled and remembered what Daniele had told me.

'It doesn't matter if you make a mistake. We stop and restart. The show must go on. You have only one shot. And keep smiling, no matter what.'

This was easier said than done. Each of the six dances I was to perform on that day had its specificities and character. I still was not one hundred per cent confident in the routines and experienced total blackouts at times. To keep smiling in those moments was an art in itself. 'Fake it until you make it,' was a popular slogan during my lessons.

'Couples, your first dance is the Samba,' the announcement came over the microphone.

Samba is my favourite Latin dance and one of the most challenging to learn. African slaves brought it to Brazil in the 19th century when they danced it on the Brazilian sugarcane plantations to distract themselves from their strenuous days of work. I love the music, which is upbeat and fun and just makes me want to move my body. Like most dances, it looks easy and effortlessly from the outside. To master the technique that requires rapid weight shifts, bouncing steps, and precise arm styling in coordination with the hip and leg movements, however, is a different game. In my lessons, Daniele often asked me to practice the arms or the hip and leg movements isolated from each other to focus on one thing only.

From my three Latin dances, I felt most confident in the Samba and the heat went well. After each dance, there is a specific routine that all the couples do: the man leads the lady into a spin before both bow to the audience to finish off the performance. In between dances, there is only a short break of maybe 15-20 seconds when the couples move to their next starting position usually walking a few steps across the floor to take a few deep breaths and mentally prepare for the next performance. Dancing is similar to acting, as each dance tells a different story, and the trickiest part is to change from one story to the next within 20 seconds.

'Your next dance is the ChaCha,' the organiser announced.

ChaCha is cheeky, fun, and playful dance with a "chase" theme between the two partners. I have found it difficult from the start, especially the coordination of the arms with the quick steps and direction changes, and was relieved that I managed to dance it without major hiccups.

Our last dance was the Rumba, the dance of love. International style Rumba music is usually slower than the American style and my biggest challenge was to stay on time with the music. The Rumba consists of two quick steps and then a third slower step that takes two beats to execute. Ballroom Rumba is a mix of slow, sensual movements and quick spins with a focus on hip movements. And because the music is slower, it takes a lot of body and leg control to convey the Rumba story.

The Rumba was our last dance in this Latin event, and we left the dance floor afterwards. I was quite happy with my performance and couldn't believe how quickly we had finished the Latin routines.

I changed into my outfit for the upcoming Ballroom events and joined the others at our table. We continued watching the other dancers. I was particularly impressed by one couple in the U21 age category. The boy was probably the same age as Max and I couldn't help thinking what if my son was dancing like that. He looked so much more mature than the young adults I knew, and I could only imagine how much time and dedication he and his partner must have put in to become such wonderful dancers.

The next event was the Adult age group (21 - 35 years) who delivered a spectacular performance with their five ballroom dances: Waltz, Foxtrot, Tango, Viennese Waltz, and Quickstep. One couple in particular stood out for me because of their poise, grace and ease they demonstrated in while swirling effortlessly across the floor. Later on, I learned that they were the current Australian ballroom champions in the Adult category.

To warm up for our four Ballroom dances, Daniele and I went back into the entrance hall to go through the routines. We then lined up at the side of the floor, again with the Masters I couples. Our first dance was the Waltz, followed by the Foxtrot and the Quickstep. Since the beginning of my dancing journey, I had always enjoyed the grand movements of these dances. When I first started dancing with Daniele, he used to say that I had so much potential in ballroom because of my height and long arm and legs. At the same time, to keep the stiff frame that requires constant rib-to-rib connection and contra-body positions is a challenge in its own.

Right at the beginning of the Waltz routine, we had a sequence of spins including the typical rise and fall and a lock step at the end to transition into a promenade sequence. I can't remember how often we had practiced that step combination and prayed to the Universe that it would work out fine. And it did! We kept walking, sliding, and spinning and across the floor with me all the way smiling. Similar to the Latin dances, except in Tango, smiling is compulsory. Even the Quickstep, my newest dance, went well. With each heat only one minute and ten seconds long, my actual dancing time in the competition was under ten minutes.

Then, it was all over and I had just danced my first ProAm competition! We returned to our table and waited for the final heats before the prize giving ceremony. As we were the only couple in Masters II, we won the competition in my age group.

On my way home, despite being physically tired, I couldn't stop smiling while I reminisced another beautiful day of dancing. I knew there were still many things to work on and improve. Daniele would surely tell me in the next lesson. It was the first step in a new chapter of my dancing journey with the next competition in four weeks and many more to follow in the future.

I reflected on 2020 and the time when we had no idea when we would be able to dance again, and, after the dance schools had reopened, when the masks would not be mandatory anymore. All the effort I had put in without knowing when we would start dancing the competitions. And if I had waited until I was perfect in all my routines, I would probably never have started at all. Perfection is the enemy of action, in any undertaking.

I was excited for my future and what I would experience and learn in the months and years ahead.

EPILOGUE
WHAT DANCING MEANS TO ME

I am so grateful that I had the courage to open that studio door for the first time in January 2018 because I quickly found that dancing is my fountain of joy. Dancing is pure energy. I love moving my body, listening to music and combining both to learn new steps or a new dance. It requires concentration and to be fully present in the moment, in other words, to be mindful. A practice that is very familiar to me from years of yoga. In 2017, it was my almost daily yoga practice and the community in the yoga studio that supported me through challenging times. In 2018, I read on the black board in the yoga studio: "Go where you find most joy." And I knew deep in my heart that this place was the dance school.

Dancing is a great way to stay fit and healthy. Samba, ChaCha or Jive are full-body workouts and have left me literally breathless more than once. Dancing requires body awareness and balance. Where is the body weight in relationship to the feet? Are the feet turned in or turned out? Do the hips move or not? What is the position of the upper body in Standard versus Latin dances? How does the head position change in Waltz, Tango, and Foxtrot depending on the lead of my partner? There are layers and layers of technique to master. I also noticed that I have become more aware of how I walk and how I hold my posture in every-day life. The teachers used to joke: 'You can tell who is a dancer when you watch people walking in the street.' More often than not, I find myself practising steps and correcting my posture in between the supermarket aisles or when I am out walking. Even in the car, I mentally repeat what I have learned in my lessons. I often practice in my living room, which has a beautiful timber floor that easily converts into a dance floor. This was especially handy during the extended lockdowns in 2020 and 2021, when I attended daily Ballroom Fit online classes.

Dancing also offers a great opportunity for socialising. Most dance studios organise monthly social dancing nights where they play a random list of songs covering everything from Waltz to Salsa. There are numerous other social dance events throughout the year focusing on specific dance styles such as New Vogue, Rock'n'Roll, Argentine Tango, and Salsa.

Apart from my personal experiences, there are many medical benefits of dancing published across the Internet. Research found that dancing reduces stress levels, increases levels of the feel-good hormone serotonin, spatial recognition, improved memory, cognitive skills, and overall brain health.

In a 2015 article, published on the Harvard Medical School website, US science writer Scott Edwards noted: "Only in recent years, neuroscience began to investigate the complex mental coordination that dance requires. Dance has such beneficial effects on the brain that it is now being used to treat people with Parkinson's disease, a progressive neurological movement disorder." In 2008, a neuroscientist from Columbia University assumed that "Synchronising music and movement, in other words, dancing, constitutes a pleasure double play. Music stimulates the brain's reward centres, while dance activates its sensory and motor circuits." The Albert Einstein College of Medicine discovered in 2003 that dance can decidedly improve brain health. The researchers looked at the impact of eleven leisure activities, such as cycling, golf, swimming, tennis, and dancing, on the risk of getting dementia. They found that only dancing lowered the risk of dementia in elderly people because "dancing involves both a mental effort and social interaction." A recipe to stay young in midlife and beyond.

A study in Frontiers in Human Neuroscience even suggests that dancing may be a better form of exercise than traditional fitness training when it comes to slowing the signs of ageing because of the added mental challenges required. These include remembering dance steps, holding your partner the right way, executing turns, recognising the beat, moving in tandem with someone, just "feeling" the rhythm of the music and moving on your own (dancing as a form of meditation), and synchronising movement with music.

Richard Powers, social dance instructor for over 40 years and full-time teacher at Stanford University's Dance Division suggests taking dance classes, which are even more effective to start building your cognitive reserve. The sooner you start, the better because "Dancing integrates several brain functions at once — kinesthetics, rational, musical, and emotional — further increasing your neural connectivity."

Dancing surely keeps my brain active. After my lessons, I often feel not only physically but also mentally exhausted. Because of my choice to learn International style ballroom dancing after two years in American Ballroom, I had to learn three new dances: Quickstep, Jive, and Paso Doble. All of them challenging in their own right. In International Ballroom and Latin all dances are choreographed routines, which we dance back-to-back on competition days. The advantage with the routines is that I know which steps or figures are coming up. The challenge is to get the routines right during the competitions. Especially in the speedy dances Quickstep, Samba, ChaCha or Jive, one mistake can throw you totally out of the game. The trick to mastery is repetition, over and over again, until the muscle memory is established.

The most important thing, however, is that dancing never fails to make me happy. After my dance lessons, I usually feel content and satisfied that I have achieved something. Science confirms that the release of the feel-good hormone serotonin after an intensive workout can simply translate into happiness. Serotonin is a vital hormone that regulates the cardiovascular and endocrine systems, appetite, sleep, memory, and mood. And the good news is that this happiness high is not a one-off situation. It is not restricted to the training session or the time immediately afterwards. Research found that the more people exercise, the more the hormone concentration in the brain grows, which leads to a sustainable improvement in concentration, more satisfaction and more happiness. That's why dancing is so addictive. The more I dance and learn, the more I want to go back to the dance floor to practise it. A virtuous circle!

I am proud that I carved out a space for myself within our family context. I could have found plenty of reasons not to do it but pushed through my doubts and have never looked back. I found something that fills up my well, an inexhaustible fountain of happiness. And often people compliment my great energy and say that they have never seen me happier. As a result, I can show up as the best version of myself for my sons, my partner, my ex-husband, my friends, business partners, and clients.

Mid-2020, I came across a video on Facebook from Dancesport Life, a community of passionate dancers with one mission: to unite the entire dance sport world. Their goal is to provide information, videos, and resources for people around the world who share the same passion: ballroom dancing. This video confirmed many of the things that I experienced and I felt even more reassured that I made one of the best decisions in my life to start dancing.

Here are five incredible character traits that dancers develop and that served me well:

1. You develop a strong work ethic.

The strong work ethic that regular practice instils, no matter how old you are, has taught me valuable skills for all areas in my life, such as grit and determination to go for my goals.

2. You become an amazing partner

Ballroom dancing has shown me what true partnership means and what it is based on: communication, respect, and trust. One of my dreams is to get more teenagers into ballroom dancing because of the social skills dancing teaches young people.

3. You become more confident

Dancing helped me increase self-confidence because it involves taking in new skills. I would not have come so far if my instructors had not regularly pushed me out of my comfort zone. It is only in the uncomfortable, a space which many people avoid, where we grow and develop ourselves personally.

4. You can express yourself freely

Dancing offers me a safe place to express myself and show my personality to the world. This requires trust in yourself and your partner. And I still often struggle with this concept, as I tend to overthink things and not let go. I realised that the more often I manage to dance from my heart and surrender, the better I feel and the happier I become.

5. You have great people around you

Looking at professional dancers, including my coach, I know they went through blood, sweat and tears to reach their goals. They are an inspiration and constant motivation to keep working on improving my dancing. And it's great to have them as friends. Not to forget the students I met along the way, a community of like-minded souls who have enriched my life.

In a nutshell, ballroom dancing can set you up for success in different areas of your private and professional life.

At 56, I have never felt more in tune with my body. I dared to dance. Sometimes I stumble and fall, yes, it happened while dancing Viennese Waltz, but I pick myself up again, enjoying my journey, because I have never felt more alive.

ACKNOWLEDGMENTS

There are a few people to whom I would like to express my gratitude because without them, this book would not have happened.

Firstly, Patti Miller, who shared her extensive knowledge with us in her life-writing classes and helped me start drafting my story in 2015. In her classes, I connected with my memoir writing group whose invaluable critiques of my chapters had a significant impact on my writing. Thank you Derice, Barbara, Clara, Bindu, and Garry for your friendship and support over the years.

I also would like to thank my father, my aunts and uncles, friends of my parents, and distant relatives who helped me shed light on our family history.

Thank you to the editors Lucy Palmer and Lliane Clark for previous manuscript assessments and advice, and to Gareth St John Thomas (Exisle Publishing) for your constructive feedback to my manuscript as part of a three-month mentorship program in 2020.

A big thank you goes to my dancer friend Kevin, who introduced me to Max Betzmeier-Wadams, my publisher. Thank you to MBW Publishing for your trust in my work and belief in my story.

And finally, most of all, I thank my Mum, who was my best friend and without whose love and support I wouldn't be what I am today. Although she left us many years ago, she continues living in me and I can see her every single day in my beautiful sons Max and Valentin.

With this book I hope to show them that they can rewrite their stories anytime in their lives.

BIBLIOGRAPHY

Aurelius, Marcus. *Meditations. Orion Books*, London, 2004.

Thich Nhat Hanh. *At Home in the World*. Rider Trade, 2016.

Li, Christine and Krautwald, Ulja. *The Path of the Empress*. Rockpool Publishing, 2012.

Everyday Mindfulness. 365 Ways to a Centred Life. Bounty Books, Octopus Publishing Group, London, 2016.

Brown, Brené. *Daring Greatly. How the Courage to be Vulnerable Transforms the Way we Live, Love, Parent and Lead*. Penguin Random House UK, 2012.

Brown, Brené. *The Gifts of Imperfections*. Hazelden Publishing, Minnesota, 2010.

Holiday, Ryan. *The Obstacle is the Way. The Ancient Art of Turning Adversity to Advantage*. Profile Books, London, 2015.

Chödrön, Pema. *When Things Fall Apart. Heart Advice for Difficult Times*. Harper Collins, London, 2005.

Hawkins, David R. *Power vs Force. The Hidden Determinants of Human Behaviour*. Hay House Inc, 2012.

Hawkins, David R. Letting Go. The Pathway to Surrender. Hay House Inc, 2012.

Hay, Louise. *The Golden Louise Hay Collection. Incl. Heal Your Body, The Mental Causes for Physical Illness and the Metaphysical Way to Overcome them*. Hay House Inc. 2012.

Singer, Michael A. *The Surrender Experiment. My Journey into Life's Perfection*. Yellow Kite Books, UK, 2016.

Shetty, Jay. *Think Like a Monk*. Simon & Schuster, US, 2020.

Tolle, Eckart. *A New Earth*. Penguin Random House UK, 2016.

Virtue, Doreen. *A Butterfly Oracle Card Set for Life Changes*.

Bernstein, Gabrielle. *The Universe Has Your Back*. Hay House Australia, 2016.

Williamson, Marianne. *A Return To Love*. HarperOne, US, 2012

Anger and Cancer: Is There a Relationship? Psychology Today, 18 September 2017